National Politics and
Sex Discrimination
in Education

National Politics and Sex Discrimination in Education

Andrew Fishel
Janice Pottker

With a chapter by

Holly Knox and
Mary Ann Millsap

Lexington Books
D.C. Heath and Company
Lexington, Massachusetts
Toronto

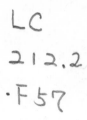

LC
212.2
·F57

Library of Congress Cataloging in Publication Data

Fishel, Andrew.
   National politics and sex discrimination in education.

   Includes index.
   1. Sex discrimination in education—United States. 2. Education and
state—United States. I. Pottker, Janice, joint author. II. Title.
LC212.2.F57   379.73   75-31291
ISBN 0-669-00336-0

Published simultaneously in Canada.

Printed in the United States of America.

International Standard Book Number: 0-669-00336-0

Library of Congress Catalog Card Number: 75-31291

For Tracy

Contents

Acknowledgments

The authors would like to express their appreciation to the people listed in the Notes section of each chapter who allowed us to meet with them during vacations, weekends, and lunch breaks, as well as after work, or who fit us into their busy workdays, in order that we could interview them. Many of these same people also contributed greatly to our research by making available to us documents they possessed that related to the events in our research. In addition, they often provided critiques on earlier drafts of the chapters, thus enabling us to benefit from their knowledge and expertise.

Particular thanks go to Holly Knox and Mary Ann Millsap for their section of this book—a chapter that could only be written by participants in the actual events described. In addition, the general interest, assistance, and enthusiasm for the book expressed by Holly Knox at all stages of the research and writing process is gratefully acknowledged.

Appreciation is also given to Howard B. Shapiro who, during the conception of this book, contributed support and valuable advice.

The authors would like to point out that this book was written in the authors' private capacity. Although two of the authors are employed by the Department of Health, Education and Welfare, no official support or endorsement by the Department of Health, Education and Welfare is intended or should be inferred.

**National Politics and
Sex Discrimination
in Education**

1 Sex Discrimination in Education Becomes a Public Policy Issue

(It was not coincidental that sex discrimination in education became a major national political issue during the 1970s.) Rather, it was the logical result of a combination of social and political factors. (At each level the educational system had been guilty of sex-role stereotyping, as well as overt and covert sex discrimination.) However, these policies and practices had gone largely unchallenged until the development of the women's rights movement. The force of this movement first brought widespread demands that schools reform the way in which they treated female students and employees.

The initial efforts by the women's rights advocates to end sexism in education were mostly aimed at educational policymakers at the local level. Feminists found that (the men who comprised the ranks of local and state education officials were uninterested, unresponsive, and unsympathetic to concerns that education policies were sex biased.) To the demands for immediate change made by these women, they were openly hostile.

At the same time that feminists saw that local and state education agency officials were apathetic to the issue of sex discrimination, they also realized that sex inequality in education was national in scope. Women's rights advocates then turned their attention to Washington. The federal government was viewed as the most likely vehicle for rapid and substantial change in the education system.

The events that transpired after 1970 in the area of federal action on sex equality in education can be better understood by reviewing some of the factors that precipitated demands for action by the federal government. A combination of circumstances transpired to act as a catalyst for the call to national action to fight educational sex discrimination. (The growth of women's rights as a social movement, combined with obvious sexism in educational policies and recalcitrant state and local policymakers, joined to bring the topic of sex discrimination in education to national attention.)

The Growth of the Feminist Movement

In the mid-1960s, no one had as yet coined the term *women's liberation movement*. The expression *sexism* was unheard of, and at the time the use of a word condemning sex discrimination that was so similar to the word *racism*, used to condemn race discrimination, would have been severely censured. The word *feminist* was in the vocabulary, although it was criticized as being as antiquated a term as *suffragist*. The term *feminist*, in the early 1960s, brought to mind a collection of elderly, well-off, educated women, now mostly widows or still spinsters, who had once helped pressure Congress for the vote for women. Feminists then, as now, received support from the organizations they formed and from governmental offices that included in their mandates concern for the status of girls and women.

Federal Government Provides Impetus for Women's Equality

The passage of the Classification Act of 1923, which equalized the pay for male and female federal workers, placed the federal government in the forefront of what would later be called an equal opportunity employer.[1] As a result of the more equitable salary schedule resulting from this Act, great numbers of qualified women over the years have sought employment with the federal government, thus creating the nucleus of support for government action on women's issues that could be tapped at a later time.

The activities of well-educated women who worked within the federal government did not include strong women's rights activities until the 1960s. However, when the women's rights movement began, these highly placed women, called "woodwork feminists" by Jo Freeman,[2] were in the right positions to help accelerate the goals of the liberation movement as it picked up speed. As a result, these women often would serve as catalysts for change on public policies affecting women.

It is not surprising that a significant portion of change agents regarding women's societal roles were those activists who were in the top ranks of female federal workers. Often forgotten when it came to promotions, yet obviously competent and extremely hard-working, these women saw their own opportunities dampened by the neglect of male bosses. They began to realize, faster than most women throughout the country, that this inattention was not personally motivated: The potential of girls and women throughout America had been ignored. These women, aided by their female colleagues in business and the professions, began to pressure for changes in the federal programs in the 1960s.

In 1961, the President's Commission on the Status of Women was established. Although it may be true as charged that this Commission, headed by Eleanor Roosevelt, was President John Kennedy's way of paying off the women in his campaign,[3] its importance lay in the fact that a Commission for women finally was formed[4] and thus made "discussion of discrimination against women intellectually respectable" for the first time.[5] It also indirectly led to the establishment of state commissions on the status of women.[6]

The Kennedy Administration's well-publicized poverty program included no job training for women, although 80 percent of those on welfare in cities were women, or children supported solely by a woman. Sargent Shriver, then head of the anti-poverty program explained the program's orientation toward men when he stated, "Why should I try to train a woman, who would rather be my wife and the mother of my children, to use a computer?"[7] Men in important national positions simply did not regard women's status as a significant factor in American life at this time. Dorothy Goldberg relates when her husband Arthur Goldberg, then Secretary of Labor under Kennedy,

. . . submitted his recommendations to the President with regard to the Commission on the Status of Women, the President looked up and said, "What's this all about?" Arthur summed up the entire case for the new Commission in one sentence, "What it says, Mr. President, is 'Are you for or agin women?' Sign here."[8]

After receiving pressure from Eleanor Roosevelt, President Kennedy issued Executive Order 10980, prohibiting discrimination in the hiring and promotion of women within the federal bureaucracy.[9] Women's groups and unions joining female legislators were later to be successful in lobbying for passage of the Equal Pay Act of 1963, which required women to receive equal pay for equal work.[10]

However, the landmark legislative action for equal rights came in 1964 with the passage of Title VII of the Civil Rights Act of 1964. This Act, prohibiting discrimination in employment, included sex as one of its characteristics. Contrary to frequently repeated accounts, sex was not added to the Act as a political maneuver to help defeat the bill, nor was it added as a joke. Congresswoman Martha Griffiths, with aid from women lobbyists, carefully planned its inclusion.[11]

In 1967, Executive Order 11246, requiring affirmative action to eliminate discrimination by employers under federal and federally assisted contracts, was issued by President Lyndon Johnson. This Executive Order later gave the Women's Equity Action League (WEAL) the basis for lodging the first demands on the national government to act to eliminate sex bias in education institutions.

President Richard Nixon, in 1969, formed a Task Force on Women's Rights and Responsibilities. The legislation that was proposed by its members touched upon diverse aspects of women's lives. Its recommendations, some of which have yet to be enacted, are generally recognized as an accurate accounting of the major sex inequities in America.

Although pressure from women workers resulted in some beneficial activities at the federal level, the issue of sex discrimination was still not treated seriously by most men in power in the 1960s. In the area of education, the topic of sex discrimination was barely raised in comparison with the great amount of attention devoted at the time to race discrimination in education.[12] In fact, the two federal agencies that should have been highly concerned with sex discrimination treated that type of injustice frivolously. The Equal Employment Opportunity Commission director in 1966, Herman Edelsberg, termed the sex provision in Title VII as a "fluke . . . conceived out of wedlock."[13] Later in the decade, Benjamin Mintz of DHEW's Office for Civil Rights stated:

We respond to social turmoil. The fact that women have not gone into the streets is indicative that they do not take employment discrimination too seriously.[14]

Although most women had not "gone into the streets" to protest discrimination, the 1960s were marked by more than just those federal policy statements made as a result of pressure from high-level federal women. Although the activities of national government officials and national interest groups began the process of change, the momentum that eventually justified and sustained these changes was derived from women advocates throughout the country. Some of the women who first latched on to the notion of sex discrimination were those who had been in the Civil Rights and New Left movement since the early 1960s. These women, usually from middle-class backgrounds, were educated, liberal, and young—characteristics that led them to perceive quickly the sex inequities in American life.

Women in the New Left

Women comprised an important segment of the New Left: They felt the same need to revolutionize society's institutions, to stop racial bigotry, and to end the war in Vietnam. Women often bore the brunt of the workload, particularly when it was tedious, uninspiring work, but were not rewarded by being made leaders in the movement.

Not only did the women provide radical men with a willing work force, they were also sexually dominated by men. No thought was given to women's rights: It was obvious that men automatically expected women to provide clerical support and sexual relations, but had no rewards for them in mind. Jerry Rubin, one of the leaders of this movement, admits: "We were as chauvinistic as the society itself, radicals as far as Vietnam and blacks were concerned, but imitation John Waynes in our personal lives."[15] This attitude towards women was reflected in Stokely Carmichael's quintessential comment regarding radical men's attitude towards radical women in this period that the only position for women in the movement was to be prone.[16]

Gradually, women awakened to the injustices that were perpetuated against them by New Left men who were acting under the guise of correcting societal injustices. When these women began calling attention to their plight in society, they were greeted with a sort of derision and scorn that made one question the entire sincerity of men in the New Left.

The men at the Students for a Democratic Society (SDS) conferences in 1965 and 1966 and at the National Conference on New Politics in 1967 threw tomatoes at the women who attempted to raise the issue of women's rights, hooted catcalls, and yelled foul obscenities at the women who raised the issue of female representation on committees.[17] (At that same conference, a black caucus demand of 50 percent representation on all committees was accepted willingly.[18]) *New Left Notes*, in 1967, depicted a woman in a baby-doll dress petulantly stating, "We want our rights and we want them now."[19] Other New Left publications of this period illustrated articles on the topic of women's rights with sexually obscene drawings of women.

It was during this period that radical women deserted the New Left, beginning the demise of this movement. Jerry Rubin states:

Women abandoned the male-dominated New Left movement, leaving men without a work force. Without women, the movement was over. Although they were dominated by men and the male image, women were the soul and heart of the movement, and often its fist, brain, and voice.[20]

Newly interested in rights for themselves, and no longer deterred by the charge that the problems of women were inconsequential, radical women joined together to create a new format for discussion. Small-group talk sessions were termed *consciousness-raising* (C-R) *groups.* In them, "women began to recognize their shared disabilities and thus discover the relevance of the liberation movement to their own situation. The process of giving testimony within a small trusted group was found to be an effective prelude to radicalizing or politicizing an individual woman's vague discontent."[21]

Much of the "vague discontent" generated in this group of women had as much to do with what society had given them as it had to do with what society had denied them.[22] Although barred from some activities—such as participating in school sports—while growing up, most of these radical women were from middle-class backgrounds that provided for them a good education and the belief that they were competent individuals. The realization that they had less of a chance of obtaining admission at certain colleges because of their sex or that certain professions were not open to them (despite their superior grades) was only perceived after a gradual process of introspection and discussion. Eventually abandoning C-R groups in order to form organizations from which to fight for their goals (sometimes the C-R group itself was turned into an organization), radical women mobilized in the late 1960s to form new groups in almost every city and college town in the country. In this time period, the women's liberation movement experienced "extraordinary growth."[23] Groups with names like Redstockings, WITCH, New York Radical Feminists, and Radical Women sprang up throughout the country. Women's Centers, places where women could find a sense of sharing and community, were established.

The movement resulted in such diverse activities as a Feminist Think Tank, a Woman's Forum, a vacation retreat for women called "A Woman's Place," and a Feminist Writers' Workshop. Nearly two hundred different feminist papers and journals were published during this period.[24] The rallying of radical women and women on campus had crystallized by the beginning of the 1970s. These young, liberal women and their fluctuating organizations were soon to be joined by a major force in American society: the working and middle-class women who constitute what most people believe to be the norm of American womanhood.

The Women's Liberation Movement
Broadens Its Constituency

Despite unflattering media portrayals, the women's movement picked up more momentum in the 1970s than was originally thought possible. Every woman could remember a time when she was put down because of her sex. That majority of women who worked outside the home only had to look at their paychecks to see proof of sex discrimination. Housewives, treated condescendingly by the very men who allegedly admired women for staying at home, began to have higher expectations for their lives. In addition, both working women and atomized housewives agreed that their daughters should have a fair chance not only for the best education available but for opportunities to enter any occupation they desired.

In order to improve society for themselves and for their daughters, women began to found new organizations that spoke to their needs more than did the radical women's groups. Equal pay, education, and legal rights were some of the early tenets of NOW, which caused great numbers of women to join. When NOW supported abortion (then illegal in most states), some women left the organization to form feminist groups with more conservative goals, as well as to form organizations more narrowly focussed on their particular interests.[25] For example, WEAL was formed to focus on fair education, employment, and taxation rights for women.[26] Professional women formed new groups, or strengthened their existing ones; The American Medical Women's Association, Sociologists for Women in Society, and the Women's National Press Club are just a few examples. Pressing for election to office was the Women's Political Caucus, which also had state organizations. Women's Lobby, Inc., pressured for federal legislation benefitting girls and women.

Ignoring charges from worried men that the women's movement reflected only the needs of white, middle-class women, labor women joined the fold by their participation in the League of American Working Women and in the newly formed Coalition of Labor Union Women, which held national conventions that were overwhelmingly attended. Also turning a deaf ear to critics who called the women's movement racially narrow in scope[27] were those women who joined the National Council of Negro Women and the National Black Women's Political Leadership Caucus.

Women active in church activities made sure that these groups, such as the National Council of Catholic Women, endorsed feminist goals such as the Equal

Rights Amendment. Nonprofessional women set up organizations like Stewardesses for Women's Rights and the National Commission on Household Employment. Even women's groups that had been in existence for many years and had never been identified in the public mind with feminism enjoyed a new surge of membership as they embraced women's new concerns. Varied groups such as the League of Women Voters, the Young Women's Christian Association, the Girl Scouts, and the Association of Junior Leagues all have endorsed feminist principles. These groups owe their success to the fact that they let women become identified with feminism while they managed to avoid a radical image and that in so doing they have been able to avert a conflict between the different roles the average woman has to play.[28]

The women's rights movement received its strength from the diverse American women who joined its ranks. Despite charges of elitism, despite the bad press image, despite lack of support from private foundations,[29] and despite the accusations that the women's movement has caused such societal problems as breakup of the family, violent crime, male impotence, juvenile delinquency, female suicide, and even lice, the women's movement has survived. Indeed, it has flourished to the point that to categorize a feminist today as a bra-burning, man-hating ugly lesbian (as she was once depicted as a few years ago) would be ludicrous.

Part of the legitimacy that the movement has gained has been due to its members' concern for their daughters' future. Some of the sympathy that men have shown towards the movement also reflects their willingness to equalize opportunities for their daughters' sake. This concern for future generations, especially in that equal education rights are stressed, reflects the importance that Americans, especially the well-educated, place on the value of education. Since so many of the women's groups members are well-educated women and since schooling is considered the key to both personal and professional success in America, it is not surprising that the focus of the women's liberation movement quickly rivetted on how girls and women were treated in education.

Sex Discrimination in Education as Public Policy

The feminist focus on schooling captured the interest of concerned teachers, parents, and students. When they began to question policies that treated males and females differently, little empirical evidence existed that supported their charges of sex discrimination in education. Instead, equal rights advocates had to rely on anecdotal evidence and personal experiences to support their claims.

However, as the topic of sex differences gained legitimacy among education researchers, and as local groups themselves became more sophisticated in how they verified their accusations, research has since been undertaken and has confirmed sex discrimination charges. The data has shown that a wide variety of educational policies and practices that are biased against girls and women exist at every level of American schooling. The extent of this problem can be seen by a review of the major areas where sex bias was alleged and subsequently proven.

Textbooks

No other aspect of sex bias in schools has received as much attention as the books used in the schools's formal curriculum. Different treatment of boys and girls, and men and women, in American textbooks is pervasive and widespread. This blatancy has made it easy to document, over and over again, the texts' unfair and inaccurate portrayal of females and males. Several historical studies have even shown that this distorted view of women has been present in texts for nearly a century.[30]

In elementary and secondary school textbooks, sexism takes many forms. Boys predominate in stories for children; they outnumber girls 5 to 2.[31] When girls are present in texts, they are almost always younger than the boys they are interacting with, which thus makes them foils for the boys' greater experience and knowledge—a situation commonly referred to as the "ninny sister syndrome."[32] Girls are shown to be far more passive than are boys and to engage in fewer activities.[33] In fact, sometimes grown women are portrayed who rely on small boys (often their young sons) to help them out of difficulty.[34]

Unbelievably, insinuating that girls are not as smart or worthy as boys is not enough; some textbooks unabashedly state it. One study found sixty-five stories that openly belittled girls (two were found that belittled boys).[35] Another study pointed out an instance where Mark, of the Harper & Row "Mark and Janet" series, states: "Just look at her. She is just like a girl. She gives up."[36] Male characters said, in another story, "We much prefer to work with men."[37] This type of material on the treatment of girls would seem to have little social or educational value, and its widespread use is difficult to understand.

Textbooks show very few types of jobs that girls might have when they grow up. One study found a ratio of women's jobs to men's jobs to be 19 to 93,[38] while another found it to be 24 to 147.[39] The occupations for women that predominate are housewife and elementary school teacher.[40] Although the majority of working women are mothers, few working mothers are shown in texts.[41] Nearly three times as many housewives exist in textbook examples as are present in American society.[42] Another study found that 63 percent of women in texts did not work.[43] Class bias is also implied in this distorted picture of occupations: Few girls of working-class families will have the economic resources to be housewives or to go to college in order to be teachers or nurses. Even the majority of those books with minority women, few of whom are housewives, show no working women.[44]

Accordingly, textbooks used in each level of American schooling are sex biased, from the preschool level[45] through graduate school.[46] This bias has also crept into different subject matter; it is present not just in readers, but in science[47] and math[48] texts, as well as social studies[49] and history[50] curricula.

Achievement and Career-Interest Tests

The purpose of career-interest tests is to help counselors measure, evaluate, guide, and place students. All too often, however, measurement tests lead to what is thought to be the student's sex-appropriate status in society rather than an accurate measurement of his or her own true interests.

The Strong Vocational Interest Blank (SVIB) and the Kuder Occupational Interest Survey (KOIS) have both been criticized for having separate sex norms for males and females; for example, when a boy and girl each have the exact same scores, they are placed, respectively, in a pre-med college course and a nursing category.[51] Because of this type of tracking, the SVIB has been called of "minimal use in counseling women about careers."[52]

Content bias against females has been found in eight major achievement test batteries.[53] Not only is item content and language usage of measurement tests partial to males, but "the pattern of stereotypic portrayal of males and females heightens and intensifies as grade level is raised."[54] Some of these tests have been found to sex-type jobs so totally that the tests seem to indicate to counselors "that sex and occupational choice are inherently related."[55] These criticisms of achievement and career-interest tests have become so widespread that guidelines have been developed by the National Institute of Education so that career alternatives not be limited by bias or stereotyped sex roles in the labor market.[56]

Counseling

At elementary school through college levels, counselors have been accused of providing girls with inferior academic, occupational, and personal guidance.[57] Analyses of counseling sessions and survey instruments show that counselors view certain jobs as being more suitable for men than for women and therefore steer girls away from these masculine occupations.[58]

Adding to this inadequate counseling for women is the counselors' lack of accurate information regarding women's participation in the labor market.[59] When asked to rate items regarding women workers as accurate or inaccurate, counselors marked over half of the items incorrectly.[60] In addition, many counselors display either negative or ambivalent attitudes toward the women they counsel: The counselors are not sure themselves what academic and occupational advice to give women.[61] Subsequent work difficulties[62] and personal problems[63] experienced by women have been attributed to this sex-typed and ineffective counseling. For all these reasons, the counseling received by women has not been responsive to the different roles women play in today's society.[64]

As a result of the stereotyped and often inaccurate responses women obtain from counselors, some women have been found to avoid seeking counseling assistance when they needed personal, academic, or occupational advice.[65]

Vocational and Career Education

Considering the bias that exists in career-interest guidance instruments and considering the current state of counseling advice, it is not surprising that vocational and career education programs have perpetuated traditional sex-role behavior patterns.[66] Fewer than 10 percent of the women in vocational education programs are being prepared for work in fields traditionally dominated by men.[67] Career content materials reinforce this sex-typing of occupations.[68] Even vocational education for handicapped children lists different jobs for men and women.[69]

Most female vocational education students are not prepared for gainful employment at all, but rather are prepared to be housewives. This situation is especially ironic in that girls who enter vocational programs are rarely from a social class background that later permits them the luxury of being housewives. Even those female students who are being prepared for work are mostly trained in fields leading to low-paying and dead-end jobs.[70] Again, girls who enter these programs will certainly find their incomes crucial for support of themselves and later as significant portions of their family incomes.[71]

In some cases where girls have wanted to enroll in a course or a program not traditionally for girls, they have been prohibited from doing so. Girls enrolled in coeducational schools have often been excluded from traditionally male fields by school policy. Not uncommonly, girls have been isolated in all-girl vocational schools that only offer a narrow range of occupational programs.[72]

Girls enrolled in regular high schools, as well as schools for the artistically or academically talented, have faced similar restrictions in terms of course enrollment and graduation requirements. For example, an extremely common practice has been for girls to be required to take home economics (and prevented from taking industrial arts) while just the opposite requirement has been established for boys. Advanced math and science classes have at times also been closed to girls if the class had insufficient spaces for all the boys who wanted to enroll. Sometimes girls have even been forbidden to attend a high school set up for the academically talented, since the school system admits only boys to it (as in the case in Philadelphia) or else requires girls to have a substantially higher grade average than boys for admittance (for example, in San Francisco).[73]

Competitive Athletics

In no other area of educational policy has such discrepancy existed in the way males and females have been treated as in competitive sports. In sports programs at both the secondary school interscholastic level and the intercollegiate level, teams for men have far outnumbered those for women, and men's teams have received much greater financial support. At the interscholastic level during the early 1970s, more than three times as many boys and girls participated on sport teams during the school year.[74] Also, more than twice the number of interscholastic high school sport teams were available for boys as for girls.[75] Even in those sports considered equally appropriate for boys as for girls, such as tennis and golf, high schools treated girls unequally. When the same sport team was offered on a separate team basis for both boys and girls, it was provided far less frequently for girls.

Because boys were offered more teams on which to participate and because greater emphasis was placed on their athletic programs, the percentage of male high school students who took part in sports was far greater than that of female students. Around 17 percent of all high school boys were on an athletic team during each season of the school year, while the participation rate for girls ranged from 1 to 8 percent of all female students, depending on the season.[76] Since the emphasis in high school sports was so heavily on boys' sports, it is not surprising that boys' teams received the greatest share of the financial expenditures for sports; the inequities in spending ratios was frequently around 10 to 1, with even greater discrepancies not uncommon.[77] It is surprising, given these fiscal inequities, that girls' parents did not until recently protest the meager share of the tax dollar that went to girls' sports.

While the treatment of girls' teams at the interscholastic level was inequitable, it still was better than that the women's teams received at the college level. Women's intercollegiate teams often received little or no financial support while extensive (almost luxurious) treatment was provided for male athletes and their teams.[78] As a result, a school like Ohio State would spend $43,000 on women's teams and over $6 million for men's teams; similar spending levels could be found at most colleges and universities.[79] According to such evidence, women's teams or women athletes were obviously not considered in most schools to be worthy of support.

Discrimination against Academic Women

Women faculty members at colleges and universities have been discriminated against in a wide number of areas. Although the exact extent to which women's inferior status in Academe is due to overt discrimination or to other factors remains unknown, the documentation available constitutes clear presumptive evidence that the low status of women in higher education is due to discriminatory attitudes and actions by male academics.

In the mid-1970s, women constituted only 24 percent of the faculty at institutions of higher education and were heavily concentrated at the lower teaching levels: 10 percent of professors, 17 percent of associate professors, 29 percent of assistant professors, 41 percent of instructors, and 40 percent of lecturers were women.[80] Furthermore, women faculty tended to be found at lower-status colleges or at two-year junior colleges. Even those women teaching at prestigious four-year colleges and universities were clustered in disciplines that have traditionally been women's fields.[81] The concentration of women in lower ranks is perpetuated by a system that keeps women at the same level for a substantially longer time period than men with equivalent qualifications.[82] This practice results in such disparities as 42 percent of the men with doctorates being made full professors, compared with only 16 percent of the women with doctoral degrees holding this rank.[83]

Not only have academic women been discriminated against in hiring and promotion, but they also have been paid less than their male colleagues for doing the same job. Estimates are that academic women as a group earn from $150 to $200 million less per year than male faculty members in comparable positions.[84] In 1975, men earned on the average more than $3,000 over what faculty women received.[85] Pay differentials exist at all ranks and at all types of institutions, thereby indicating that the discrepancy could not be entirely explained due to different wages paid at different ranks and at different types of schools.[86]

Women have also been treated unequally in their teaching assignments and the granting of tenure. Women faculty members generally have been given the least desirable teaching assignments in that far more women teach only undergraduate classes than is true for men. In contrast, far more male faculty have only graduate classes to teach.[87] Women are also less likely to have tenure than male faculty. Around 60 percent of men, but only 42 percent of women, had tenure in 1975.[88]

State and Local Education Officials Are Unresponsive to Demands for Change

Because education is primarily a local function and responsibility, initial criticisms of sex bias in the education system were directed at policymakers at this level. However, the domination of local education positions by men, and the attitudes held by these officials, made achieving change at the local level extremely difficult. State education officials were no more inclined than local policymakers to make the changes demanded by concerned parents, students, and faculty.

At the local level, all key policy positions have been held, overwhelmingly, by men. While in 1973, 66 percent of the 2,110,368 public school teachers in the country were women, only 13.5 percent of the principals and 12.5 percent of the assistant principals were women.[89] Almost all of the women (95 percent) who were principals held this position at the elementary school level. Indeed, the number of women serving as principals has been declining steadily and rapidly for over fifty years. By 1973, women constituted only 20 percent of the elementary, 3 percent of the junior high, and 1 percent of the high school principals in the country, and women were nearly as poorly represented at the assistant principal level.

A popular rationalization for appointing men rather than women as principals has been that men are better suited and more capable to be principals. However, numerous studies conducted over the past twenty years comparing the various aspects of the behavior and performance of men and women principals have proven this assertion to be inaccurate.[90] In fact, these behavioral evaluations clearly indicate that in terms of ability to supervise and administer a school and to maintain good relations with students and parents, the few women who have been able to obtain administrative positions have performed as capably, if not more capably, than male administrators.

Studies such as these lend support to the belief that prejudiced attitudes rather than the women's lack of ability are the reason they have not been appointed to administrative positions. In fact, many people believe that the criteria used to recruit and hire principals has often not been related to the skills and characteristics needed to be an effective administrator and that sex, rather than ability, has been the determining factor in appointments to principalship positions.

Since women have rarely been appointed to principalships, it is not surprising that few women have become local superintendents of school. The fact that in 1973 99.9 percent of all local superintendents, 94 percent of all deputy and associate superintendents, and 95 percent of assistant superintendents were male indicates that few of the women who managed to get appointed principals advanced any farther in the organizational hierarchy; in 1973 only 65 out of 13,037 local superintendents were women.[91]

Women are not only poorly represented in professional positions at the local level but few are on lay boards of education. Many people assume that since women traditionally have been active in education, they would be well represented on local boards of education. In reality, the percentage of women on school boards has hovered between 10 and 15 percent from 1920 to the mid-1970s.[92] By the early 1970s, only 12 percent of the nearly 100,000 local school board members were women and over half of the boards in the country did not have any women members.[93] Furthermore, those women who did manage to be elected or appointed to a board often found that they could not be effective in this position due to the patronizing and condescending attitudes of the male board members with whom they served.[94]

Since two-thirds of public school teachers are women, it might be thought that the leadership of local teacher organizations would be dominated by women and that these organizations would work hard to represent the interests of their women members. However, this has not usually been the case. Local teacher organizations have generally been controlled by male teachers and have used their influence and the collective bargaining process to advance salary and working condition policies that primarily benefit male teachers. In addition, inequitable policies toward women in such areas as pay for extracurricular activities, maternity leave policies, and cost and benefits from pension plans have been developed with the direct involvement and full support of these organizations.[95]

At the state level the situation is similar to that at the local level: Few women are in decision-making positions. For example, in 1972 only one state had a woman chief state school officer, and in only four states was a woman a deputy associate or assistant state superintendent.[96] Women were not significantly better represented at the next level of leadership in state departments of education: Only 9 percent of the office directors were women. In terms of the lay state boards of education, 20 percent of the members of these bodies were women, while five states had no women members and fifteen others had only a lone woman represented.[97]

At the state level, men also dominated teacher associations. In 1973 only 15 percent of state education association presidents were women, and no state had a woman acting as executive secretary. Of the entire professional and semi-professional staffs of these associations, only 14 percent of the positions were held by women.[98]

The underrepresentation of women in key education posts is also a characteristic of institutions of higher education. Women rarely are appointed to the position of department head or to other administrative posts. In 1970, only 11 percent of college presidents and 4 percent of vice-presidents were women, and these almost always were at women's colleges. Similarly, fewer than 20 percent of academic deans were women.[99] The boards of trustees that oversee colleges and universities are also dominated by men. Twenty-one (21) percent of these boards had no women on them and another 25 percent had only a token woman.[100] Since women trustees have been found to react more positively to demands for change,[101] the absence of women from college governing boards undoubtedly contributed to the unsympathetic reception that reforms for treatment of women students and faculty received.

The underrepresentation of women in local and state education policy-making positions would not have been a major deterrent to eliminating sex bias in the schools if the male leaders had been more sensitive to the issues raised as a result of the women's rights movement and more receptive to the demands for change. However, this was not the case. For example, even after repeated criticism and extensive documentation that textbooks were sex biased, a substantial portion of school administrators did not believe there was anything wrong with the textbooks used in their school district. In 1972, 84 percent of administrators throughout the country did not think that curriculum materials were sex biased.[102] Not only did they not accept the charges against the text, they rejected the claims made without even bothering to investigate the validity of the claims; only 17 percent of administrators indicated that they had made an effort to review textbooks regarding their portrayal of women. The poll produced comments such as "Sex bias? Hogwash" and "Just a figment of some feminist's frustrated imagination."[103]

In 1973, a similar poll of school administrators found that nearly a quarter of these local education officials rejected the charge that girls' athletic programs were shortchanged in favor of boys' programs.[104] As stated earlier, numerous studies have found that superintendents and school board members oppose appointing women to administrative positions and often object to having them serve on school boards.

A 1974 poll of state government and state education officials found that sex bias in education was not even a major issue for these state leaders.[105] The poll found that state leaders considered equalizing opportunities for women in education their fifteenth most important education issue out of eighteen issues facing them.

Confronted with local and state education policymakers who were unsympathetic to the plight of women students and teachers, combined with the knowledge that the federal government had often been in the forefront of the movement to achieve equal rights for women as well as other minorities, feminists became increasingly interested in obtaining government action at the national level to help end sex discrimination in education. While the federal government institutions were as controlled and heavily dominated by men as the local and state institutions, a major difference existed in Washington. By the end of the 1960s Washington had a small but growing number of highly qualified and motivated women who worked in the Department of Health, Education and Welfare, Congress, or various national interest groups who were interested in and concerned about sex discrimination in education.

These women, working with sympathetic men, would use the executive, legislative, and judicial processes of the national government during the early and mid-1970s to help challenge policies that discriminated against women employed as teachers and school administrators, and against girls and women who were enrolled as students. The events involved in four of the major efforts to eliminate sex discrimination in education by federal governmental action are chronicled in the following chapters.

Notes

1. Kathryn G. Heath, "Legislation and Its Implications for Elimination of Sex Bias," *Journal of the National Association for Women Deans, Administrators and Counselors* 37 (Winter 1974), p. 60.

2. Jo Freeman, *The Politics of Women's Liberation* (New York: David McKay, 1975), p. 228.

3. Barbara Deckard, *The Women's Movement: Political, Socioeconomic, and Psychological Issues* (New York: Harper & Row, 1975), p. 325.

4. Judith Hole and Ellen Levine, *Rebirth of Feminism* (New York: Quadrangle Books, 1971), p. 24.

5. Catherine East, *Chronology of the Women's Movement in the U.S. 1961-1975* (Washington, D.C.: National Commission on the Observation of International Women's Year, Department of State, 1975), p. 1.

6. Freeman, *Politics*, p. 10.

7. Betty Friedan, *It Changed My Life* (New York: Random House, 1976), p. 79.

8. Dorothy Goldberg, *A Private View of A Public Life* (New York: Charterhouse, 1975), p. 259.

9. Caroline Bird, *Born Female* (New York: David McKay, 1968), pp. 45-46.

10. East, *Chronology*, p. 2.

11. Ibid.

12. Heath, "Legislation," p. 64.

13. Freeman, *Politics*, p. 54; Hole and Levine, *Rebirth*, p. 34; and Bird, *Born*, p. 5.

14. Freeman, *Politics*, p. 79.

15. Jerry Rubin, *Growing (Up) at 37* (New York: Evans and Co., 1976), p. 89.

16. Freeman, *Politics*, p. 57.

17. Editorial Research Reports, *The Women's Movement* (Washington, D.C.: Congressional Quarterly, Inc., 1973), p. 14; Maren Lockwood Carden, *The New Feminist Movement* (New York: Russell Sage Foundation, 1974), pp. 59-62; Freeman, *Politics*, pp. 57-60; and Hole and Levine, *Rebirth*, pp. 110-14.

18. Hole and Levine, *Rebirth*, p. 112.

19. Freeman, *Politics*, p. 58.

20. Rubin, *Growing (Up)*, p. 89.

21. Editorial Research Reports, *Movement*, p. 16.

22. Cynthia Fuchs Epstein, "Ten Years Later: Perspectives on the Women's Movement," *Dissent* 22 (Spring 1975), pp. 169-76.

23. Hole and Levine, *Rebirth*; and Roberta Salper, "The Development of the American Women's Liberation Movement, 1967-1971," *Female Liberation*, ed. by Roberta Salper (New York: Knopf, 1972), pp. 169-84.

24. Freeman, *Politics*, p. 27.

25. East, *Chronology*, p. 5.

26. Hole and Levine, *Rebirth*, p. 96.

27. Cynthia Fuchs Epstein, *Reflections on the Women's Movement* (New York: Institute of Life Insurance, 1975), p. 19.

28. Carden, *New Feminist*, p. 107.

29. Mary Jean Tully, "Funding the Feminists," *Foundation News* 16 (March-April 1975), pp. 24-33.

30. Sara Zimet, "Little Boy Lost," *Teachers College Record* 72 (September 1970), pp. 31-40; and Joan Burstyn and Ruth Corrigan, "Images of Women in Textbooks 1880-1920," *Teachers College Record* 76 (February 1975), pp. 431-40.

31. Women on Words and Images, *Dick and Jane as Victims* (Princeton, N.J.: Women on Words and Images, 1972).

32. Joan Beck, "Feminist Movement Hits Children's Books," *Chicago Tribune*, December 14, 1974.

33. Ramona Frasher and Annabelle Walker, "Sex Roles in Early Reading Textbooks," *Women and Education*, ed. by Elizabeth Steiner Maccia (Springfield, Ill.: Charles Thomas, 1975), pp. 226-38.

34. Janice Pottker, "Psychological and Occupational Sex Stereotypes in Elementary School Readers," *Sex Bias in the Schools: The Research Evidence*, ed. by Janice Pottker and Andrew Fishel (Cranbury, N.J.: Fairleigh Dickinson University Press, 1976), pp. 111-25.

35. Women on Words, *Dick and Jane*, p. 32.

36. Celeste Brody, "Do Instructional Materials Reinforce Sex Stereotyping?" *Educational Leadership* 31 (November 1973), pp. 119-22.

37. Betty Levy and Judith Stacey, "Sexism in the Elementary School: A Backward and a Forward Look," *Phi Delta Kappan* 55 (October 1973), pp. 105-09, 23.

38. Pottker, "Sex Stereotypes," pp. 111-25.

39. Women on Words, *Dick and Jane*, p. 40.

40. Ibid., p. 74.

41. Frasher and Walker, "Sex Roles," p. 228.

42. Pottker, "Sex Stereotypes," pp. 111-25.

43. Buford Stefflre, " 'Run, Mama, Run' Women Workers in Elementary Readers," *Vocational Guidance Quarterly* 18 (December 1969), pp. 99-102.

44. Delores Prida and Susan Ribner, "Feminists Look at the 100 Books: The Portrayal of Women in Children's Books on Puerto Rican Themes," *Sexism and Youth*, ed. by Diane Gersoni-Staun (New York: Bowker, 1974), pp. 272-88.

45. Lenore Weitzman, "Sex Role Socialization in Picture Books for Preschool Children," *American Journal of Sociology* 77 (May 1972), pp. 1125-49.

46. Diane Scully and Pauline Bart, "A Funny Thing Happened on the Way to the Orifice: Women in Gynecology Textbooks," *American Journal of Sociology* 78 (January 1973), pp. 1045-50.

47. Levy and Stacey, "Sexism," pp. 105-09.

48. Winifred Tom Jay, "Sex Stereotyping in Elementary School Mathematics Textbooks," in *Sex Bias in the Schools: The Research Evidence*, ed. by Pottker and Fishel, pp. 124-45; and Marsha Federbush, "The Sex Problems of School Math Books," in *And Jill Came Tumbling After*, ed. by Judith Stacey, et al. (New York: Dell, 1974).

49. Richard O'Donnell, "Sex Bias in Primary Social Studies Textbooks," *Elementary Leadership* 31 (November 1973), pp. 137-41; and American Association of School Administrators, *Sex Equality in Educational Materials* (Arlington, Va.: AASA, 1975), pp. 6-7.

50. Janice Trecker, "Women in U.S. History High School Textbooks," *Sex Bias in the Schools: The Research Evidence*, ed. by Pottker and Fishel, pp. 146-62.

51. Carol Tittle, "Sex Bias in Educational Measurement: Fact or Fiction?" *Measurement and Evaluation in Guidance* 6 (January 1974), pp. 219-26.

52. Carol Huth, "Measuring Women's Interests: How Useful?" *Personnel and Guidance Journal* 51 (April 1973), pp. 539-49.

53. Carol Tittle, "Women and Educational Testing," *Sex Bias in the Schools: The Research Evidence*, ed. by Pottker and Fishel, pp. 257-74.

54. Terry Saario et al., "Sex Role Stereotyping in the Public Schools," *Harvard Educational Review* 43 (August 1973), p. 402.

55. Lenore Harmon, "Sexual Bias in Interest Measurement," *Measurement and Evaluation in Guidance* 5 (January 1973), pp. 499-500.

56. Esther Diamond, ed., *Issues of Sex Bias and Sex Fairness in Career Interest Measurement* (Washington, D.C.: N.I.E., 1975).

57. Gary Walz, ed., *The Counselor and the Feminine Protest*, December 1971, ERIC, Arlington, Va.

58. John Pietrofessa and Nancy Schlossberg, "Counselor Bias and the Female Occupational Role," *Sex Bias in the Schools: The Research Evidence*, ed. by Pottker and Fishel, pp. 221-29; Joann Gardner, "Sexist Counseling Must Stop," *Personnel and Guidance Journal* 49 (May 1971), pp. 705-08; and H. Thomas and N. Stewart, "Counselor Response to Female Clients with Deviate and Conforming Career Goals," *Journal of Counseling Psychology* 18 (1971), pp. 352-57.

59. J.M. Birk, J. Cooper, and M.F. Tanney, "Racial and Sex Role Stereotyping in Career Information Illustration," paper presented at the American Psychological Association Annual Meeting, Montreal, August 1973.

60. William Bingham and Elaine House, "Counselors View Women and

Work: Accuracy of Information," *Sex Bias in the Schools: The Research Evidence*, ed. by Pottker and Fishel, pp. 239-46.

61. William Bingham and Elaine House, "Counselors Attitudes Toward Women and Work," *Sex Bias in the Schools: The Research Evidence*, ed. by Pottker and Fishel, pp. 247-56.

62. Dorothy Haener, "The Working Woman: Can Counselors Take the Heat?" *Personnel and Guidance Journal* 51 (October 1972), pp. 109-12.

63. Joyce Smith, "For God's Sake, What Do Those Women Want?" *Personnel and Guidance Journal* 51 (October 1972), pp. 133-36.

64. Jane Berry, "The New Womanhood: Counselor Alert," *Personnel and Guidance Journal* 51 (October 1972), pp. 105-08; John Hipple, "Perceptual Differences in Concepts of the Ideal Woman," *The School Counselor* 22 (January 1975), pp. 180-86; Laurel Oliver, "Counseling Implications of Recent Research on Women," *Personnel and Guidance Journal* 53 (February 1975), pp. 430-37; John Parrish, "Women, Careers and Counseling: The New Era," *Journal of the National Association for Women Deans, Administrators and Counselors* 38 (Fall 1974), pp. 11-19; and Lewis Patterson, "Girls Careers—Expression of Identity," *Vocational Guidance Quarterly* (June 1973), pp. 269-75.

65. Judith Lewis, "Counselors and Women: Finding Each Other," *Personnel and Guidance Journal* 51 (October 1972), pp. 147-50.

66. Jo Ann Steiger and Sara Cooper, *The Vocational Preparation of Women: Report and Recommendations of the Secretary's Advisory Committee on the Rights and Responsibilities of Women* (Washington, D.C.: HEW, 1975); Pamela Roby, "Toward Full Equality: More Job Education for Women," *School Review* 84 (February 1976), pp. 181-211; Janice Trecker, "Room at the Bottom: Girls Access to Vocational Training," *Social Education* 38 (October 1974), pp. 533-608; Shirley McCune, "Vocational Education: A Dual System," *Inequality in Education* (March 1974), pp. 28-33; and Andrew Fishel and Janice Pottker, "Sex Bias in Secondary Schools," *Sex Bias in the Schools: The Research Evidence*, ed. by Pottker and Fishel, pp. 92-104.

67. Steiger and Cooper, *Vocational Preparation*.

68. Lois Heshusius-Gilsdorf and Dale Gilsdorf, "Girls are Female, Boys are Males: A Content Analysis of Career Materials," *Personnel and Guidance Journal* 54 (December 1975), pp. 207-11.

69. Patricia Gillespie and Albert Fink, "The Influence of Sexism on the Education of the Handicapped," *Exceptional Children* 41 (November 1974), pp. 155-62.

70. Angelo Gillie, Sr., "Women in Vocational Education," *American Vocational Journal* 49 (November 1974), pp. 34-36.

71. Elizabeth Simpson, "Vocational Education Can Lead," *American Vocational Journal* 49 (November 1974), pp. 37-38.

72. Fishel and Pottker, "Sex Bias in Secondary Schools," pp. 94-104.

73. Commissioner's Task Force on the Impact of Office of Education Programs on Women, "Segregated Academic and Vocational Schools: Separate But Not Equal," *Sexism and Youth*, ed. by Gersoni-Staun, pp. 88-89.

74. Janice Pottker and Andrew Fishel, "Separate and Unequal: Sex Discrimination in Interscholastic Sports," *Integrated Education* 14 (March-April 1976), pp. 3-7.

75. Ibid.

76. Ibid.

77. Ibid.

78. Bill Gilbert and Nancy Williamson, "Sport is Unfair to Women," *Sports Illustrated* (May 28, 1973), pp. 80, 90-8; Ellen Weber, "Revolution in Women's Sports," *Women Sports* (September 1974), pp. 36-38; Project on the Status and Education of Women, *What Constitutes Equality for Women in Sport?* (Washington, D.C.: Project, 1974); and Brenda Feigen Fasteau, "Giving Women a Sporting Chance," *Ms.* (July 1973), pp. 56-58, 103.

79. Weber, "Revolution," pp. 36-38.

80. "Women Faculty Lose a Little Ground, NCES Reports," *Higher Education Daily* February 2, 1976, pp. 3-5.

81. Everett Ladd, Jr. and Seymour Lipset, "Faculty Women: Little Gain in Status," *Chronicle of Higher Education* (September 29, 1975), p. 2.

82. Lora Robinson, "Institutional Variation in the Status of Academic Women," *Academic Women on the Move*, ed. by Alice Rossi and Ann Calderod (New York: Russell Sage Foundation, 1973), p. 208.

83. Alice Rossi, "Status of Women in Graduate Departments of Sociology," *The American Sociologist* 5 (February 1970), p. 6.

84. "Making Haste Slowly: The Outlook for Women in Higher Education," *Carnegie Quarterly* 21 (Fall 1973), p. 50.

85. "Women Faculty Lose," *Higher Education Daily*.

86. Robert Dorfman, "Two Steps Backward: Report on the Economic Status of the Profession, 1974-75," *AAUP Bulletin* 61 (August 1975), pp. 118-24.

87. National Center for Educational Statistics, *Digest of Educational Statistics, 1972* (Washington, D.C.: U.S. Government Printing Office, 1973), p. 91.

88. "Women Faculty Lose," *Higher Education Daily*.

89. Andrew Fishel and Janice Pottker, "Women in Educational Governance," *Sex Bias in the Schools: The Research Evidence*, ed. by Pottker and Fishel, pp. 505-13.

90. Andrew Fishel and Janice Pottker, "Performance of Women Principals:

A Review of Behavioral and Attitudinal Studies," *Sex Bias in the Schools: The Research Evidence*, ed. by Pottker and Fishel, pp. 289-99.

91. Fishel and Pottker, "Educational Governance," pp. 505-73.

92. Andrew Fishel and Janice Pottker, "School Boards and Sex Bias in American Education," *Sex Bias in the Schools: The Research Evidence*, ed. by Pottker and Fishel, pp. 311-19.

93. Ibid.

94. Carolyn Mullins, "The Plight of the Board Woman," *The American School Board Journal* 159 (February 1972), pp. 27-32.

95. Andrew Fishel and Janice Pottker, "Women Teachers and Teacher Power," *Sex Bias in the Schools: The Research Evidence*, ed. by Pottker and Fishel, pp. 277-88.

96. Fishel and Pottker, "Educational Governance," pp. 505-13.

97. Ibid.

98. Fishel and Pottker, "Women Teachers," pp. 277-88.

99. Ruth Ottman, "Women in Academic Governance," *Sex Bias in the Schools: The Research Evidence*, ed. by Pottker and Fishel, pp. 514-24.

100. Ibid.

101. Rodney T. Harnett, "Characteristics and Attitudes of Women Trustees," *Sex Bias in the Schools: The Research Evidence*, ed. by Pottker and Fishel, pp. 411-14.

102. "Schoolbook Sex Bias: Seek and Ye Shall Find," *Nation's Schools* 91 (December 1972), p. 18.

103. Ibid.

104. Kathleen Engle, "The Greening of Girls' Sports," *Nation's Schools* 92 (September 1973), p. 27.

105. Education Commission of the States, *State Education Priorities: A Poll of State-Level Education Policymakers* (Denver: ECS, 1974), p. 3.

2

Sex Discrimination and the Judicial Process: The Cohen v. Chesterfield County Maternity Leave Case

"I feel I have been dealt with unfairly and have been penalized for telling the truth."[1] It was this straightforward belief of Susan E. Cohen that triggered the events that culminated in a landmark Supreme Court decision regarding the rights of women. At the time of Susan Cohen's lawsuit, almost all American school districts required a pregnant teacher to leave the classroom somewhere in her fourth, fifth, or sixth month of pregnancy. Many also mandated that the teacher could not return to work until her child was one or two years old.[2]

Background to the Case

To the casual observer, Susan Cohen, who describes herself as being very middle class and not active in the women's liberation movement, is an unlikely source for a major constitutional test of a women's rights issue such as maternity leave. Cohen began teaching at Midlothian High School in Chesterfield County, located in suburban Richmond, Virginia, in the fall of 1968. Cohen, twenty-six years old at the time, had spent almost all her life in New York City: first, growing up in the Bronx, then receiving her B.A. in history from C.C.N.Y., and later teaching in the New York City public school system while earning a M.A. degree from Teachers College, Columbia University. When Susan Cohen's husband, Leo was accepted in a doctoral program at the University of Virginia, she, like many women, exchanged one teaching position for another in order to follow her husband to his new location.

Cohen threw her energies into teaching her American government classes and earned recommendations from school administrators, students, and parents for her total commitment to both the social and intellectual development of her students. Although uninvolved with any type of community groups or teacher associations, she had shortly earned the reputation of being a dedicated teacher and was an accepted member of the community. The school officials were happy to have her as a teacher, and she was equally happy to be teaching in a friendly, pleasant school system. In short, she had what was considered to be a perfect work situation.

Although Cohen had been thinking for several years about having children, it was not until she moved to Chesterfield County that her plans crystallized. She had always assumed that she could stay in teaching while pregnant and based her unquestioned belief that the idea of requiring a capable teacher to

23

quit work due to pregnancy was totally illogical. Without investigating what the maternity leave policy in Chesterfield County was, she became pregnant in late summer of 1970. She planned to teach through nearly all of the school year and to stop at the earliest at the end of the six-week marking period in March 1971, which was shortly before her child was due in the beginning of May. She had also planned to notify the school district of her pregnancy by the end of the third month, as Chesterfield County policy dictated.

Cohen never worried about the possibility that after informing the school district of her pregnancy, she would be out of a job. But her friends were more savvy than she: They told her not to notify the school of her pregnancy as early as the policy required, and to lie about her due date. Since Cohen experienced no illness due to pregnancy and was so small that she did not begin to wear maternity clothes until her sixth month of pregnancy, concealing facts from school personnel would have been an easy way to continue teaching a few months longer. But Cohen objected and said that she was a valuable teacher and if she played it straight and complied with all the school rules, there was no logical reason why she could not teach for as long as she desired.

Being careful to conform with every school policy, she notified the district of her pregnancy and, following regulations, included a note from her obstetrician stating that she was healthy and perfectly capable of teaching until the date of confinement. Cohen was not sure whether the district would let her teach until her child was born in late April or early May, but she was certain she would be allowed to stay in the classroom until the end of the six-week marking period in March.

According to the Chesterfield County policy manual, a pregnant woman may teach through her fifth month, and an extension may be granted if the physician, teacher, principal, and superintendent concur, as long as it is in the students' best interest. The policy stated:

Termination of employment of an expectant mother shall become effective at least four months prior to expected birth of the child. Termination of employment may be extended if the Superintendent receives written recommendations from the expectant mother's physician and her principal, and if the Superintendent feels an extension will be in the best interest of the pupils and schools involved.[3]

Cohen Protests School Policy

Susan Cohen clearly wanted to continue teaching, and her physician agreed that there was no reason why she could not stay in her job. Also important to Cohen was the fact that her students were seniors, many of whom were college-bound, and that their switching teachers during senior year at any time other than shortly before graduation would be unfair to them since their grades were so important. It seemed to Cohen that all that remained for her to do was to obtain her principal's recommendation to remain in the classroom, since the tradition within the school district was that the superintendent follow the principal's recommendation regarding date of commencement of maternity leave.

Cohen approached her principal in October 1970 and told him of her desired termination date of April 1971. The principal, a recent arrival to the school district, told her that that date was, in his opinion, unsatisfactory. His stated reason for requiring teachers to leave the classroom well ahead of their due date was because his wife, when pregnant, delivered earlier than expected.

Serious in its implication for all teachers was the fact that expert medical advice was given no credence by the policymaker. The recommendation of Cohen's physician that she be allowed to continue teaching until April 1 obviously carried less weight than the principal's personal opinion—based on the experience of his wife—that pregnant women should not continue to work.

The principal told Cohen that she should write the assistant superintendent requesting the April 1, 1971, termination date she preferred. However, her principal proposed to the assistant superintendent that January be the final date of employment.

Although Cohen was not happy about the prospect of having to leave at the end of the fall semester in January 1971, she was totally unprepared for the letter she received from the assistant superintendent giving December 18, 1970, as her termination date. Cohen was upset and hurt at having been given what she felt was a run-around by her supervisors, and she was concerned and worried that she was being forced to leave a short time before the crucial senior mid-year exams and grades were to be given.

At this point, Susan Cohen had given up all hope of staying in teaching until April; for the sake of her students, she now just wanted to be allowed to remain until the end of January. When pressed, the principal could give Cohen no reason for why she had to leave in the middle of December instead of in January.

Cohen, trying to make some sense of the situation, contacted the superintendent of schools, then in his second year with Chesterfield County. Since neither the principal nor the assistant superintendent were, in Cohen's opinion, following the county's policy recommendations regarding maternity leave, Cohen read aloud to the superintendent the maternity regulations. Cohen emphasized that it was illogical to require her to leave in December, and certainly not in the students' best interests.

The superintendent responded repeatedly that requiring her to leave on that date was "policy" and increasingly frustrated, apparently at his own lack of intelligent reply, blurted out that after all Cohen "might die tomorrow."[4] The altercation ended when the superintendent said that she should send her request to remain in her job to the school board. Without her knowledge or involvement, the school board at its next meeting voted without any discussion to deny Cohen's request. Upon learning this action had been taken, Cohen became furious and contacted the superintendent. The superintendent told Cohen that he would allow her to appear at the next board meeting to present her argument in person, but added that the school board always goes along with his recommendation.

Shortly before meeting with the school board in November 1970, Cohen contacted the local teacher organization, Chesterfield Education Association (CEA), which was a local member of the National Education Association (NEA). CEA was a somewhat obscure organization to most teachers in that it did not have the power to negotiate teacher contracts with the Chesterfield County school system. This lack of power meant that its impact was negligible, and as a result, few Chesterfield teachers were active members.

Due to the lack of bargaining power of the local CEA, Susan Cohen had never joined this organization. She did turn to them for assistance, however, before the board hearing. Unfortunately, all they could recommend was that she go to see the assistant superintendent with their representative. Since she had already taken this step by herself, she was not interested in repeating it. The CEA replied that there was nothing else that they could do for her.

Cohen did receive support from students and parents regarding her decision to fight the superintendent's policy. Because she was afraid that parental involvement would merely hurt her chances before the board, she asked the concerned parents who called her not to take any steps on her behalf. Susan Cohen tried not to be the type of person who could be termed a *troublemaker*: She believed that by telling the truth and following procedure, her interests would be best served.

One evening in November 1970, Susan Cohen spent thirty minutes facing a group of school board members who were all white, all male, and all middle aged or older. Several men were in their seventies; in fact, one man was so old that he could not remember his precise birthdate. The superintendent was also present.

Cohen tried to act as polite and deferential as possible under the circumstances, so as not to antagonize these men. Again, she did not put on an act for their benefit; although she was riled, she is basically a teacher who would not challenge authority unless she thought her rights were being abridged.

The attitudes of the board members towards her seemed fatherly and paternal: Clearly they thought they were acting in her personal best interest, but again did not take account of her physician's letter, which stated that working while pregnant was not harmful. She also received the impression that the members thought it unseemly to have a noticeably pregnant teacher in the classroom.

The board members informed her that it was necessary for them to act in the best interests of the students. She again explained that to bring in a new teacher, unfamiliar with the course curriculum or with each student's work, and to have this new teacher compose a final exam and decide semester grades for seniors was far from being in the students' best interest. Cohen also explained that the time from December 18 and the end of the semester was only ten school days, and not even ten teaching days. Approximately four days were teaching days and six were exam days. She asked the superintendent why it was so important for him to deny her these ten extra work days when these days were crucial to her students. A board member angrily interjected, "Who do you think you are, to cross-examine the superintendent of schools?"

Shortly after this harsh outburst, one board member made a motion to deny Susan Cohen her request, which was then immediately adopted by unanimous vote. Cohen stalked out of the room, furious and on the verge of tears. She was mostly frustrated because she believed her treatment to be undeserved; she thought that she was being penalized for telling the truth. The school would not have known she was pregnant if she had not informed them of it. She believed that she had fulfilled each step that the policy required for a maternity extension and still had been denied on the vague and arbitrary grounds of "policy."

What Cohen did not know at the time was that the school district, upon hearing of her pregnancy, had begun the process of hiring a teacher to replace her. This was easy enough to do since the school district had a waiting list of applicants for social studies teaching positions. Since the district had hired a replacement before her termination date, they probably were especially eager for Cohen to vacate her position.

Cohen Begins Legal Action

Soon after the board's action, Leo Cohen repeated Susan's experiences and feelings of injury to a friend, who mentioned that he knew a young lawyer, John B. Mann, who would be interested in hearing about this situation. Mann was fresh out of law school and still unemployed when he was introduced to Susan and Leo Cohen. Mann had received his B.A. degree from Duke University and his L.L.B. degree from George Washington University and had always been interested in civil rights work. When he told the Cohens that legal remedy might be available to them, he took on the first case he ever handled, and he did this for them at no fee.

Although a young inexperienced lawyer may not appear to have been the best choice as attorney for the type of legal test that Cohen entered into, the fact that Cohen could find any lawyer to handle her case should not be taken for granted. Women teachers in other parts of the country seeking to challenge the legality of maternity policies at this time were often unable to obtain any legal counsel since many lawyers saw the maternity issue as trivial or could not see any grounds on which these policies could be challenged. As a result, Mann's insight into the potential use of constitutional grounds to challenge sex discrimination must be considered unusual and perceptive.

However, the overall grounds of sex bias were not Cohen's concern, as she merely wanted her job back. Not being aware at that time of how these maternity leave issues impacted on women as a class, Cohen went into litigation out of personal anger. In fact, if the school board had only allowed her to remain teaching for ten more days, until the semester break in January, she never would have contested the legality of the district's maternity leave policy.

In December 1970, John Mann asked the U.S. district court in Richmond, Virginia, to issue a preliminary injunction that would reinstate her to a teaching position until her case against the school board could be heard. Cohen stated that she would not be able to find employment until the next teaching year, and that she would also lose seniority by leaving before the end of the semester. So inexperienced was Mann that he was not even a member of the federal bar at the time: Court had to be opened especially for him and a clerk found to swear him in so that he would be eligible to file suit in Cohen's behalf.

The preliminary injunction was denied in early January by Judge Robert R. Merhige, Jr., on the grounds that no irreparable harm would be done to Cohen by being dismissed. Her seniority and monetary damages could be compensated by court action at a later point, and although her students could be damaged by her absence from the classroom, they were not clients to the suit. It was not surprising to Mann that the injunction was denied. Although Mann and Cohen were disheartened by their failure to put Cohen back in the classroom, they were still optimistic about winning their case, since the decision on the request for an injunction did not take into consideration the merits of the actual charges being brought against the school board's maternity leave policy.

The suit filed by Mann on Cohen's behalf against Chesterfield County challenged the legality and constitutionality of the maternity leave policy on several grounds. Specifically, Mann charged that the school board, by arbitrarily terminating Cohen's employment because she was pregnant, violated the due process and equal protection guarantees in the Fourteenth Amendment. Mann also mistakenly charged the board with violating Title VII of the Civil Rights Act of 1964, although Title VII at this time specifically excluded public employees from coverage.[a]

After filing suit on Cohen's behalf, John Mann contacted an attorney he knew from his involvement with ACLU while in law school. Philip J. Hirschkop presented a background of almost impeccable credentials for any case resembling that of Susan Cohen, since Hirschkop was nationally active in ACLU and had also been on retainer in the late 1960s as chief litigator for the Du Shane teacher's rights fund of NEA. Hirschkop had racked up an impressive and

---

[a]Title VII was subsequently expanded by Congress in 1972 to cover public employees, and the Equal Employment Opportunities Commission, which administers the implementation of Title VII, was to issue guidelines mandating that maternity leave be treated in the same fashion as other leaves of absence for temporary disabilities. However, since Cohen's legal action began before Title VII was amended to cover public employees, her case was not affected by the change in federal law.

extensive range of court victories in the areas of civil rights, women's rights, prisoners' rights, and teachers' rights.

Hirschkop encouraged Mann in his belief that there were solid grounds for the Cohen case and agreed to step in and give Mann assistance and also to contact NEA to gain financial support of their legal action. Hirschkop then spoke with representatives at NEA's Du Shane Fund in the national office in Washington about the Cohen case, even though he did not consider it to be the perfect test case.

The Du Shane Fund, begun in 1934 as a fund-raising campaign to assist in teachers' rights cases, had by the 1960s grown along with NEA so that it now has a yearly budget of nearly two million dollars. The main funding source is membership dues; one dollar of the dues collected from each NEA member currently results in today's Du Shane budget of about 1.8 million dollars. The Du Shane fund works from an advocacy position to protect and defend teachers' rights. It is reactive in that it does not usually seek out circumstances from which to bring suit; nearly all future litigants contact the Du Shane fund themselves.

NEA showed an immediate interest when Hirschkop called. After all, Phil Hirschkop had a perfect litigation record for them, since he had never lost a teachers' rights case. When apprised of their interest, Cohen sent in the standard Du Shane application form for aid. Normal procedure, which consists of the application being approved by Du Shane staff and then by the NEA's Office of General Counsel, followed. Since Cohen's case met the stricter standards for funding that a non-NEA member like Cohen must meet—that the case both set precedent and benefit the teaching profession as a whole—it was approved for funding. Although Hirschkop's advocacy of Cohen's case certainly carried weight at NEA, the teacher's organization was definitely interested in the issue of maternity leave on its own merits as well.

By this time, the discovery period for the district court trial was nearly up, and much work of gathering evidence remained. Hirschkop left his Alexandria, Virginia, law office to travel several hours to Chesterfield County in order to take the depositions, with Mann, from Chesterfield's school board members. At this point, Mann became Hirschkop's cocounsel, doing legal research work but leaving the future courtroom oral arguments to Hirschkop. The rationale for this stemmed from both the logical reasoning that Hirschkop had greater experience in arguing in court and greater knowledge of court procedure, and also from the desire of NEA that the more proven attorney present the case in court.

In order to help them learn the motivations of the Chesterfield school board members when they developed the school district's maternity leave policy, Hirschkop and Mann used the period after filing suit and prior to the actual trial to obtain statements on the issue from each board member. (These depositions proved to be crucial evidence for Cohen at every level of the case.)

When Mann and Hirschkop took depositions from the board members, it seemed to Cohen's attorneys that the Chesterfield County school system was still not taking Cohen's policy complaint seriously. The board members had been in no way prepared by their own attorney for questioning as to policy motives for their maternity regulations. Their attitude seemed to be one of assurance that they would win and seemed to be based on a strong trust in the right of school boards to make unquestioned policy decisions.

Cohen's attorneys also believed that a major error in judgment was committed by the board's attorney when he permitted each member to be questioned by Hirschkop separately. All board members were entitled to be present during the taking of depositions as parties to the suit, which would have allowed each board member to hear the questioning and testimony of other members and would have thus made it possible for the remaining members to organize and synchronize their thoughts. Their failure to reject separate questioning is another example of how the case was not treated by the school board as a serious threat to their policy. Possibly, however, the fact that Cohen lost her motion for a preliminary injunction encouraged the board to have a false expectation of victory.

Although there were few uniform answers to the rationale of the Chesterfield County maternity policy, several types of reasoning were advanced by the board members. Every board member save one, stated that his medical knowledge of pregnancy stemmed from what he remembered about pregnancy when his wife was pregnant. A typical statement was, "I think from what my wife went through I would say four months is a good time [to terminate employment]."[5] All members admitted having never asked for medical advice regarding teaching during pregnancy when formulating policy.

To Cohen and her counsel, such statements indicated that public policy was being made by men who had no greater knowledge of, nor experience with, pregnancy except that their wives had been pregnant. It also should be noted that according to their depositions, none of the board members' wives worked during pregnancy, nor did they work afterward. In fact, some members' wives had never assumed a life role other than that of housewife. Although these members were able to identify with their pregnant wives, it seemed obvious that these men would find it difficult to identify or sympathize with a professional woman who thought she had a right to practice her chosen career.

One of the depositions came from a board member born in 1892. This seventy-eight-year-old, an eighteen-year veteran of the Chesterfield County school board, believed that pregnant women should not teach ". . . because some of the kids say, my teacher swallowed a watermelon."[6] He apparently believed that this would be the reaction of Susan Cohen's seniors in 1971. This concern for teacher appearance, however, was not limited to one member. Vague references to pregnant teachers not looking right in the classroom were made, thus possibly making the board member's statement regarding a watermelon in the stomach the only truly honest response in this issue.

The taking of the depositions represented the first major record of the case. Hirschkop and Mann knew that the board had a weak case due to their different answers regarding reasons for policy decisions given during the deposition taking. At this point, Hirschkop thought that, due to lack of procedural problems, the chances of winning the district court case were overwhelmingly in Cohen's favor.

The brief submitted for Cohen was written by Mann with David Ross Rosenfeld, a clerk in Hirschkop's office. It presented extensive legal arguments challenging the district's maternity leave policy. The issue, as presented in the legal brief, primarily asked the court to decide whether the rights of due process and equal protection of the laws under the Fourteenth Amendment should be accorded to women as a class. Hirschkop and Mann hoped to expand the definition of what constituted a *suspect classification*, a legal term that had been used for years to protect the rights of racial minorities and that Cohen's attorneys hoped would be eventually extended by the courts to protect women as well.

Therefore, the attorneys presented arguments in their brief to justify the conclusion that any classification based on sex should be considered constitutionally suspect and allowed only if there was a compelling state interest for the classification. According to this reasoning, if a government policy had to meet this stricter scrutiny for how a policy affected women as class, then many policies that would have been allowed if sex were not considered a suspect classification would then be prohibited. If the use of sex as a category only had to meet the more standard test that there be a rational basis for public policy, then policies that treated women differently from men might continue to be considered legally permissible.

The District Court Trial

The case of *Cohen* v. *Chesterfield County School Board* was heard in U.S. district court before the Honorable Robert R. Merhige, Jr., in April 1971. Merhige is considered one of the better district court judges regarding constitutional matters. In fact, one of the reasons that NEA was optimistic about supporting the Cohen case was because it knew the case would be heard by Judge Merhige.

Merhige seemed both receptive and interested throughout the hearings.[7] The attorney for the school board at the district court was the commonwealth attorney who handled civil matters for Chesterfield County. He was not experienced as a federal litigator, and apparently realizing this, had previously tried to have the case heard in state court, especially since these courts are not as stringent about enforcement of the federal constitution. Merhige was, in fact, constantly critical of this attorney for his lack of proper courtroom demeanor, as well as impatient with the defendants for the lack of merit in their arguments.

John Mann called Susan Cohen, who was in her last month of pregnancy at this time, as his first witness. In her testimony, she emphasized that she had never been ill due to pregnancy and that she was more physically active while unemployed than she had been while teaching. The board's attorney, in cross-examination, questioned Cohen on such seemingly irrelevant points as how fast she could run while pregnant and what position she slept in at night.

The next witness Mann called was Cohen's obstetrician, who stated that most problems of pregnancy subside after the first trimester and that unless a woman was employed as a riveter, there was no reason to have her cease work during pregnancy. He also denied, during cross-examination, that women are less stable mentally while pregnant. (Judge Merhige may have paid particular attention to this witness's testimony, since this physician was the obstetrician who delivered Merhige's own children.)

Shortly before the district court hearing, Hirschkop had contacted Catherine East, executive secretary of the federal Citizens' Advisory Council on the Status of Women (a presidential council), to testify as an expert witness. Hirschkop knew East as a witness from another women's rights case he had argued. He believed that having worked for the federal government, most recently in the area of the status of working women, she was a perfect witness. The Citizens' Advisory Council was the only organization to have developed a comprehensive position on maternity leave that made a distinction between child bearing and child rearing and advocated that the disabilities associated with delivery and complications of pregnancy be treated by employers like all other disabilities. East had developed the evidence and rationale for the Council's recommendation, which was later adopted by the Equal Employment Opportunity Commission as its interpretation of Title VII of the Civil Rights Act of 1964.

East presented evidence that showed a very low rate of absenteeism due to pregnancy, especially as compared with absences due to common health problems such as respiratory illness, and she emphasized that special provisions for employment of pregnant women are not protective of these women, as employees have stated, but rather hurt them. East was to leave this courtroom to testify the next day at the U.S. district court in Cleveland, in the similar maternity leave case of *La Fleur* v. *Cleveland Board of Education*, a case whose history was to interact with Cohen's from the district court to the Supreme Court level.[b]

---

[b]Jo Carol La Fleur and Ann Nelson were junior high school teachers in Cleveland. When Nelson became pregnant during the 1970-71 school year she was required by the school board to resign five months before the birth of her child. La Fleur was required when she became pregnant during the same school year to take a five-month unpaid leave of absence and was told she could not return to work until the second semester in the 1971-72 school year. Both women left the school system in the middle of the semester in March, 1971. La Fleur and Nelson filed separate suits in the northern district of Ohio challenging the school board's regulation on the ground that it violated the equal protection clause of the Fourteenth Amendment. The district court tried the cases together and rejected the

After the lunch recess, the first witness called on behalf of the school board was the head of the Chesterfield Education Association (CEA), who Susan Cohen had previously consulted in November for advice on going before the school board. He testified that he and other CEA members had drawn up a recommended maternity policy and presented it to the Chesterfield board. The only difference between the CEA policy and the school board's policy was that the teacher be evaluated before going on leave. Otherwise, the CEA policy completely supported the requirement that a pregnant woman leave teaching by the end of the fifth month of pregnancy. Under reexamination the CEA representative admitted that the committee had not obtained any medical advice before formulating this policy. In fact, CEA's policy had been drafted by a group of members who were mostly male, although only 20 percent of Chesterfield County teachers were men.

The local CEA policy was contradictory to policy of the NEA, the national organization. In fact, NEA's official and financial support of Susan Cohen showed that they were diametrically opposed to their local's stance. The CEA policy was actually formulated when several teachers, prior to Cohen's dismissal, were required by the school board to leave teaching due to pregnancy. When these teachers asked for assistance from their local organization, CEA supported the board's policy rather than the teachers.

The school board's next witness was the Chesterfield County fire chief. The purpose of his testimony was to show that a pregnant teacher could not run out of a burning building as quickly as a nonpregnant teacher and could thus endanger students' lives. Judge Merhige appeared less than impressed with this reasoning when he pointed out that he thought that one should walk, not run, in case of fire.

The last witness for the defendants was Robert F. Kelly, school superintendent. Kelly's testimony supported the school board's position that Cohen had signed a contract and was therefore obligated to follow this contract. Most of his testimony regarded continuity of instruction, with his stating that letting pregnant teachers in the classroom past the fifth month of pregnancy would be detrimental to continuity of instruction.

It was on the issue of continuity of instruction that Merhige personally interrupted and questioned Kelly carefully, by asking what was "magic" about requiring women to leave in the fifth month of pregnancy rather than the third or seventh. He also questioned the reluctance of the board to have noticeably pregnant teachers in the classroom by asking: "Are we way back in the Middle Ages where there was some stigma of obscenity to a perfectly natural, normal, wonderful thing."[8] (Since in the depositions most board members had said that

teachers' argument, but on appeal a divided sixth circuit reversed the district court's ruling and held that the Cleveland policy did violate the equal protection clause. (See *La Fleur* v. *Cleveland Board of Education*, 326 F.Supp. 1208 [N.D. Ohio 1971] and 465 F.2d 1184 [6 Cir. 1972].) The Cleveland Board of Education subsequently appealed to the Supreme Court where this case was consolidated with the Cohen case.

they deferred to the superintendent on policy matters, it was crucial to examine the superintendent for the reasoning behind the policy.) Hirschkop, on cross-examination, also caused Kelly to admit that the continuity-of-instruction argument that he was stating as rationale for the policy was a recently conceived idea: In Kelly's original deposition, the superintendent never mentioned continuity as the explanation for the maternity policy.

It was obvious to both of her lawyers by the end of the day that Susan Cohen would win her case. They believed that the school board did a very poor job of bolstering the continuity-of-instruction argument, that it should have brought in a physician as a witness for the defense, and that it was not best served by the attorney it had chosen. It would have been to the board's advantage to have hired a lawyer especially for the case who was more knowledgeable about federal court procedure and who was more skilled at being a procedural obstructionist, since cases such as Cohen's are often lost due to procedural issues rather than on the merits of the case. In fact, Merhige did not even let the board's attorney finish his closing statement; he said to him during his closing argument "It doesn't sound like you and I heard the same case."[9]

In May 1971, District Court Judge Merhige handed down his decision in favor of Cohen. Merhige concluded that there was no medical reason for the board's regulation. He reasoned that since no time projections were alike, decisions on when a pregnant teacher should discontinue working should be left to the woman and her doctor. Merhige concluded that the dates contained in the Chesterfield maternity policy were arbitrarily selected without a rational basis, and as such the policy discriminated on the basis of sex in violation of the equal protection clause of the Fourteenth Amendment. The judge ordered the board to pay Cohen back salary and to grant her seniority credit for the time she was not allowed to teach. In short, it was a complete victory for Cohen as well as a major advance for women's rights under law since the court had accepted the argument that sex be considered a suspect classification equivalent to race when considering charges of discrimination.

Community Reaction

By the time of the district court trial in April 1971, the Richmond area community had been made aware of the Cohen controversy by local newspapers. Parents and students at Midlothian High School had known for almost six months, however, of Cohen's termination due to pregnancy and had made their support of Susan Cohen well-known to school officials.

In January 1971, after Cohen's dismissal, Cohen's warning to school administrators about what would happen if she were forced to leave before the end of the semester came true; her replacement was unable to compose the semester exam for his senior students. The principal actually went to Cohen's former department head and requested him to ask Cohen to write the final exam. When called by her past department head, Cohen reminded him that according to the school she was not capable of writing an exam at this point in pregnancy. The department head was forced to go into school files for Cohen's old exams and to use the questions from these for the seniors' test.

Although the community in no way ostracized Cohen, local feeling was not very empathic. Aside from Cohen's students' parents, who did not want their children to lose a good teacher, most people believed that Cohen was making a fuss over a superficial issue. Many were not sure whether it looked proper for a visibly pregnant woman to teach, while others thought that working while pregnant might be physically harmful to a woman or her unborn child. Also discouraging to Cohen was the typical attitude held by attorneys in the town that maternity leave was a trivial issue.

Student interest ran high by the time of the district court hearing. The students showed their support of Cohen by placing her picture in the student lounge, with the inscription "Our Hero" under it. Many also wanted to attend court, which must have infuriated the principal who stated that anyone missing school due to court attendance would be suspended. Some of Cohen's former pupils who were now in college did take the time to come back to Richmond for the hearings. Cohen's principal could not have been too happy with the following newspaper report of the district hearing: "Mrs. Cohen looking chipper and drawing support from some of her present and former students who listened with rapt attention. . . ."[10]

Most local papers' accounts were not so favorable as this, however. Although their negative comments were largely and properly confined to editorials and did not influence news reporting, the cumulative effect of consistently adverse editorials must have affected local feelings. An editorial published shortly after the contradictory Cohen decision in favor of the teacher and the *La Fleur* v. *Cleveland* district court decision in favor of the school board stated: "It seems to us the Ohio decision is the more logical one and more in the interest of an orderly and effective educational process."[11]

Chesterfield County Appeals District Court Decision

As far as Phil Hirschkop was concerned, Cohen's victory at the district court level closed the case. It seemed evident that the school board's treatment of Susan Cohen was clearly wrong: It was beyond reason to treat pregnant teachers as they did. But Chesterfield County, encouraged by the Cleveland district court decision in favor of the school board, filed a brief in September 1971 in the U.S. Court of Appeals for the Fourth Circuit, which appealed the earlier decision of the district court. While it was appealing, Chesterfield County refused to change the policy struck down by the district court.[c]

Chesterfield County switched attorneys for their appeal and retained a man who was a former attorney general of Virginia and current state senator. The general reasoning behind the change in lawyers seemed to be a realization by the board that they had lost and they had better do something about it. Hiring a more savvy lawyer was their apparent response.

Mann and Rosenfeld again prepared the brief for Cohen, with Hirschkop acting as their adviser by overseeing and reviewing the brief-writing process. In January 1972, Hirschkop argued the case before a three-member appellate court panel that included Chief Judge for the Fourth Circuit Clement Haynsworth, Jr., who had received national attention several years earlier when President Nixon's nomination of him for the Supreme Court was rejected by Congress because the members considered him unqualified. The other judges on the panel were Harrison Winter, a circuit judge, and Joseph Young, a district judge. Ironically, one of Young's law clerks was pregnant at the time of the argument.

In their argument, the school board basically attempted to show that their maternity leave policy was not so devoid of any reasonable basis that it violated the equal protection clause of the Fourteenth Amendment. They emphasized that they were not discriminating against women, but rather between all teachers and those teachers who happen to be pregnant: "The fact of pregnancy, rather than sex, is the focus of the regulation."[1 2]

Arguing that the main reason for the maternity policy was to foster continuity in the educational process, and stating that pregnancy unlike other medical conditions had a "unique predictability" as to termination date, the board attempted to show that their regulation requiring teachers to leave at a fixed date in pregnancy was not arbitrary, but rather that it was reasonable. A rehash of formerly stated rationale was presented, including the question: "Must the school board await a fire in a school and injury to a teacher in her eighth month of pregnancy who cannot negotiate a crowded hall of excited students before a regulation requiring maternity leave at the end of the fifth month has a rational justification?"[1 3]

The brief for Susan Cohen argued that the Chesterfield County policy discriminated on the basis of sex in violation of the equal protection clause, by pointing out that the board's argument of pregnancy, rather than sex, being at issue was ludicrous unless the board knew of any pregnant men. They noted that no other type of medical disability was treated as stringently by the board as was pregnancy. This also indicated that the lack of medical evidence showed the board's regulation to be without rational basis and that this absence proved that the board's regulation did not constitute a compelling state interest.

---

[c]By appealing the decision, Chesterfield County effectively discouraged other teachers who had been forced to take maternity leave from also filing suit for their lost incomes. By the time the case was finally decided, the time limitation for filing suit against the county had passed for many teachers who had previously been forced to take leave, thus preventing them from obtaining damages.

Although by the time of the filing of these briefs in the fall of 1971, the Equal Employment Opportunity Commission (EEOC) regulations that treated pregnancy as a temporary disability were still only in effect for private employees (public employees were not covered until 1972), the Commission's expertise and advice was sought by Cohen's attorneys. In response to their request, EEOC filed an amicus curiae (friend of the court) brief. (It is common for an organization or institution such as EEOC, while not personally involved in a suit, to file an amicus brief to support a legal point raised in a case that could influence the institution. It is also not unusual for an agency of the federal government to file an amicus brief, especially in a civil rights case.)

The EEOC brief argued that the school board's maternity policy discriminated on the basis of sex, since only women become pregnant. It also stated that the board policy violated the equal protection clause of the Fourteenth Amendment, by declaring that sex should be identified as a suspect classification and therefore be subject to strict scrutiny. Also mentioned was the necessity of judging pregnant women according to their individual ability, as well as the board's failure to bolster its continuity of instruction objective. "It is difficult to evaluate that concern [of maintaining continuity in the classroom], however, where, as in this case, the school board itself insists upon disruption of continuity by compelling teachers to leave in the middle of the semester. This is hardly a model of action rationally related to the objective."[14]

In their brief replying to the argument presented by Cohen and EEOC, the school board argued that even if their regulation made a classification based on sex, there was no support for extending the strict scrutiny test, since strict scrutiny applies only to cases involving race or national origin.[15]

The U.S. Court of Appeals for the Fourth Circuit affirmed the previous district court decision for Cohen by 2-1 on September 14, 1972, more than one full year after the Chesterfield board had appealed. Mentioning the board's argument of the necessity for a fixed leave date in order to further continuity of instruction, Judge Winter, in writing the opinion and joined by Judge Young, stated: "While superficially appealing, we think this argument lacking in merit and indeed a disingenuous one to be advanced on this record."[16] Continuing, the court noted: "And on the facts of this case, we can reasonably infer that continuity of the educational process would have been better preserved had Mrs. Cohen been permitted to complete the semester, rather than to subject her students to a new teacher at an illogical and avoidable breaking point in the curriculum."[17] Agreeing that the board policy was discriminating to women as a group since only women become pregnant, the decision stated: "But there is a more fundamental defect in the school board's argument. That the regulation is a discrimination based on sex, we think is self-evident."[18]

In addition, the court agreed that the Chesterfield regulation denied equal protection: "The record is literally devoid of any reason, medical or administrative, why a pregnant teacher must accept an enforced leave by the end of the fifth month of pregnancy if she and her doctor conclude that she can perform her duties beyond that date."[19] Furthermore, the fourth circuit court of appeals noted that it was in agreement with the recent (July 1972) court of appeals decision in the sixth circuit in the similar case of *La Fleur* v. *Cleveland Board of Education*, which also held the Cleveland maternity regulation invalid as a denial of equal protection.

Judge Haynsworth dissented, by stating that the Chesterfield maternity regulation was not an invidious discrimination based upon sex: "It does not apply to women in an area [pregnancy] in which they may compete with men."[20] Continuing, he stated: "The fact that only women experience pregnancy and motherhood removes all possibility of competition between the sexes in this area. No manmade law or regulation excludes males from those experiences, and no such law or regulation can relieve females from all of the burdens which naturally accompany the joys and blessings of motherhood."[21]

Haynsworth claimed that pregnancy is unlike a temporary disability because pregnancy is voluntary.[d] "No one wishes to come down with mononucleosis or to break a leg, but a majority of young women do wish to become pregnant, though they seek to select the time for doing so. Female school teachers, like other young women, plan to become pregnant."[22]

By this time, winning came as no surprise to Cohen or her attorneys. Susan Cohen, having moved out of Virginia before the appeals hearing, again felt satisfied that she had proven her point to the school board but was not particularly emotionally elated. She was disinterested, after the district court decision, in the further legal maneuvering her attorneys were engaged in and accurately believed that her involvement at this point was inconsequential, especially since her attorneys thought they were assured of victory.

En Banc Decision

Absolute amazement was the reaction of Cohen's lawyers to the resubmission of the appellate decision in January 1973 for consideration, en banc, by the entire seven-member bench of the fourth circuit court of appeals.[e] In its en banc

---

[d]The supposed distinction between a "voluntary" temporary disability and an "involuntary" temporary disability has been used often in conjunction with maternity leave cases, usually to women's disadvantage. It has been claimed in these cases that pregnancy is voluntary and therefore not a temporary disability. Pregnancy, however, is not always voluntary. In addition, many other types of temporary disability for which leave or disability pay is granted could be defined as voluntary or caused by a voluntary activity: plastic surgery, breaking a leg while skiing, vasectomy, venereal disease, emphysema caused by smoking, and so forth.

[e]Cases decided at the appellate level are generally reheard en banc only if the case involves: a technical flaw in the appellate court hearing; an extremely important issue on which the appellate decision was split; or an issue on which major legal developments have occurred since the original appellate decision was handed down. Since none of these factors applied to the Cohen case, the lawyers for Cohen did not believe that the holding of an en banc hearing was warranted.

decision, the fourth circuit court voted 4-3 to reverse the district court's ruling and uphold the Chesterfield County maternity leave policy. Justice Haynsworth was joined by the other Republicans on the court in supporting the view he had written originally as dissenting minority appellate opinion. The three Democrats on the fourth circuit court of appeals all supported the original appellate opinion in Cohen's favor.

The decision that resulted went against the legal precedent that had been established by this time in Cohen's favor. In light of the facts, which included La Fleur's victory in the sixth circuit court of appeals and many lesser court rulings for pregnant teachers, Haynsworth's majority decision seemed unbelievable to Cohen's lawyers. The en banc decision was a reflection of the composition of the fourth circuit court and showed the conservatism of those on the bench. There may have been an equally strong factor to contend with here, however. Along with the notation that the Chesterfield County school board attorney was Haynsworth's former law clerk, strong courthouse rumors, which were circulated after this unusual en banc hearing, indicates that Haynsworth lobbied to have a rehearing of this case and then railroaded through his opinion.

Although Susan Cohen, John Mann, and Philip Hirschkop had never expected the case against Chesterfield County school board would ever be heard before the Supreme Court, after the en banc decision, there was no question but that they would petition for a Supreme Court hearing. Since the sixth circuit appellate court had already ruled in La Fleur's favor, the contradictory ruling in the fourth circuit practically guaranteed that the Supreme Court would hear the case since it would not want to leave a situation where two circuit courts had decided the facts of similar cases in different ways. Cohen's attorneys were convinced that due to the statements that they had received in the beginning of litigation from the Chesterfield superintendent and board members, they had an excellent chance for a favorable ruling by the Supreme Court. But if it had not been for the contradictory ruling in the sixth circuit, the case may never have been accepted by the Supreme Court; the final decision would have been that of the appellate court.

Preparation for the Supreme Court Hearing

Hirschkop and Mann petitioned to have Cohen's case heard before the Supreme Court in the October term of 1973, one year after the fourth circuit appeals court decision and nine months after the fourth circuit's en banc decision. In their petition for writ of certiorari, Cohen's attorneys put forth their reasons why the writ should be granted and the case heard before the Supreme Court. Mentioning the decision of the sixth district court in *La Fleur*, the writ stated that the Chesterfield policy constituted an arbitrary and invidious sex classification in violation of both the due process and the equal protection clauses of the Fourteenth Amendment.

The Supreme Court agreed to hear the case of Susan Cohen versus Chesterfield County in the fall term of 1972, along with the case of *Cleveland Board of Education* v. *La Fleur* where the school board had appealed the adverse decision of the appellate court. When the Supreme Court accepted her case, Cohen became the first teacher in the country to challenge maternity leave policies before the Supreme Court. John Mann and David Rosenfeld worked on Cohen's Supreme Court brief at Hirschkop's office. Again, Hirschkop acted as senior counsel. Cohen's case did not involve a large expenditure of time at this point, due to the fact that there was not a large record and that the issues were clear-cut; in all, it was an easy case to bring before the Court.

There was little coordination between Cohen's attorneys and La Fleur's attorney, Jane Picker of the Women's Law Center of Cleveland. However, a massive effort was made by the three attorneys and by NEA to encourage and coordinate the filing of amicus curiae briefs. Since the lawyers and the Du Shane staff at NEA were sophisticated and experienced in civil rights and teacher rights, they knew which organizations to contact.

Before the filing of these briefs, a large meeting was held at NEA, attended by over a dozen different attorneys working for the various organizations filing amici briefs, as well as NEA's own general counsel staff. This group met in order to sort out the question of which briefs should present the different arguments and cover the various points. Some of the people at the meeting were concerned primarily with women's rights, while others were basically teachers' rights advocates.

The filing of an amicus brief by an organization is an important act, both in terms of its symbolic value and in terms of the facts that support a particular case. The amicus briefs filed in support of Cohen represented diverse organizations and varied interests. The United States entered as amicus curiae due to the Department of Justice and the Equal Employment Opportunity Commission's responsibility for enforcement of Title VII under the 1964 Civil Rights Act. Any court ruling on issues similar to EEOC regulations would therefore be of consequence to these agencies.

Interest groups, such as the American Civil Liberties Union, AFT, The American Jewish Congress, the National Organization for Women (NOW), National Education Association, and Women's Equity Action League, also filed amici briefs. NEA's amicus brief (and to a lesser extent, AFT's amicus brief) was of great importance to Cohen's case in that it showed the Supreme Court that the recognized authorities in the teaching profession supported Cohen; it dispelled the argument of the Chesterfield board that Cohen was a lone dissatisfied teacher protesting this policy; and most important, it showed the board's continuity of educational instruction argument to be weak.

Amicus curiae briefs were filed on behalf of the Chesterfield County and Cleveland school boards by the states of Virginia and California. The state of California entered because of its concern that the resolution of this case could affect the issues raised in a pending case before the Supreme Court that concerned disability insurance for maternity leave.

Delta Air Lines and the U.S. Chamber of Commerce also filed as amicus curiae for the school boards. The filing of the Delta brief was not surprising since there were a great many maternity leave suits pending against Delta Air Lines as well as other commercial airlines.

These four amicus briefs appeared uncoordinated in their content and did not present nearly as impressive array of documentation as did the amicus briefs filed on Cohen's behalf. The Delta and Chamber of Commerce briefs actually seemed somewhat gratuitous—that is, the organizations seemed obliged to submit briefs but apparently did not expend much effort in trying to influence the Court in a teachers' rights case. Delta and the Chamber of Commerce were obviously concerned with the potential impact of the Court's decision on business maternity leave policies and had little interest in the education or teachers' rights aspects of the case.

It was obvious that the school boards did not undertake the same coordination of amicus briefs that parties supporting the teachers had done. The boards could have contacted other state and local school boards and asked them to submit amicus briefs on their behalf and indicated how harmful a ruling for Cohen would be from their perspective. Their failure to do so would seem to indicate a lack of understanding regarding the significance of challenges to teacher maternity policies on the part of the school boards, since the ruling in Cohen's and La Fleur's cases would affect every school district in the county. Yet the Supreme Court case appeared to be treated quite casually by the very education officials it would directly influence.

Supreme Court Hearing

The case of *Cleveland Board of Education* v. *La Fleur* was heard in the morning of October 15, 1973, and after a lunch recess, the attorneys for Cohen and for Chesterfield County spent the total alloted time of fifty minutes presenting their oral arguments before the Court.

Hirschkop was not able to present the full argument he had prepared as the justices interrupted and asked questions regarding points that interested or concerned them. Hirschkop emphasized the board depositions and pointed out the emphasis placed on appearance of teachers and the lack of any medical rationale for the maternity policy. He also argued that this policy does not further continuity of instruction.

The Chesterfield County attorney, in what seemed to be a less than impressive argument, tried to justify mandatory maternity policies. The justices continually asked him to explain how continuity of instruction was served by requiring a teacher to leave at the end of the fifth month of pregnancy. One justice stated: "It does not make any difference so far as your continuity argument goes, whether the teacher leaves after four months of pregnancy, or after eight months, or after eight months and three weeks of pregnancy."[23] One particularly weak argument advanced by the board was that pregnant women frequently have to visit their physician, and that this interferes with their teaching duties. A justice asked: "Is there something peculiar about Chesterfield County that they only hold doctors' services while school is in session?"[24]

In rebuttal, Hirschkop experienced more difficulty than he had previously. He was questioned closely on which aspects of the policy violated the equal protection clause. Chief Justice Burger and Justice Rehnquist asked him to state a medical disorder experienced only by males, similar to pregnancy for females. Feeling boxed in by their questions, Hirschkop was unable to immediately give them an analogous male disorder. Hirschkop later could not recall the specific Chesterfield County policy involved since he had been spending much of his time prior to the oral presentation working on a class action suit challenging 160 maternity policies in Virginia schools. Instead, he referred the justices to the record of the case regarding the policy in question.

Hirschkop saw that when he argued the case based on equal protection grounds, he was more closely examined than when he presented the due process argument. However, it was difficult to tell what the justices were thinking regarding a legal basis for their ruling. Hirschkop was worried after the oral argument that due to the paucity of sex discrimination cases, there was not a strong enough record for the justices to rule on equal protection grounds. It also appeared conceivable that the Court would not have been willing, no matter how strong the record, to base a ruling on the grounds of equal protection. In any case, the firing of questions at Cohen's attorney at the end of the argument left them unsure as to the intention of the justices, and uncertain as to what the final decision would be.

It was announced in January 1974 that the Court in a split 7-2 decision ruled that the mandatory termination provisions of the Chesterfield County maternity policy (and of the Cleveland maternity policy) violated the due process clause of the Fourteenth Amendment.[f] In its decision, the Court noted that as long as a teacher gives advance notice of pregnancy, arbitrary cut-off dates have no valid relationship to the state's interest in maintaining continuity

---

[f]The Court also ruled that the Cleveland policy requiring a woman to stay out of teaching for at least three months after childbirth was unconstitutional. The Court described this provision as wholly arbitrary and irrational and stated that it unnecessarily penalized women for having children. The Chesterfield County return policy, in contrast, was upheld. By requiring the teacher to wait to return to teaching until the beginning of the next school year, the Court stated that the goal of continuity of instruction was being achieved. Among the other issues resolved by the Court was the right of school boards to: require a teacher to provide substantial advance notice that she is pregnant; require a doctor's certificate of a woman's ability to continue working during pregnancy and to return to work after childbirth; and to require a statement from the teacher that she would devote full attention to her job.

of instruction. In delivering the opinion of the Court, Justice Stewart noted that "the present Cleveland and Chesterfield County rules may serve to hinder attainment of the very continuity objectives that they are purportedly designed to promote."[25] The Court also noted that due process is violated when the school board assumes that all pregnant women are unable to teach.

We conclude, therefore, that neither the necessity for continuity of instruction nor the state interest in keeping physically unfit teachers out of the classroom can justify the sweeping maternity leave regulations that the Cleveland and Chesterfield School Boards have adopted. While the regulations no doubt represent a good-faith attempt to achieve a laudable goal, they cannot pass muster under the Due Process Clause of the Fourteenth Amendment, because they employ irrebuttable presumptions that unduly penalize a female teacher for deciding to bear a child."[26]

Justice Stewart delivered the opinion of the Court, in which Justices Brennan, White, Marshall, and Blackman joined. Justice Douglas concurred in the result, and Justice Powell filed an opinion concurring with the result, but stating that the equal protection grounds should have been used to justify the decision. He indicated that the equal protection clause has been disguised here as a due process doctrine and stated: "The constitutional difficulty is not that the boards attempted to deal with this problem by classification. Rather it is that the boards chose irrational classifications."[27]

Justice Rehnquist filed a dissenting opinion, in which Chief Justice Burger joined. The dissenting opinion was based on dissatisfaction with the majority opinion's questioning of classifications that treat all people within that classification in the same manner:

All legislation involved the drawing of lines, and the drawing of lines necessarily result in particular individuals who are disadvantaged by the line drawn being virtually indistinguishable for many purposes from those individuals who benefit from the legislative classification. The Court's disenchantment with "irrebutable presumptions," and its preference for "individualized determination," is in the last analysis nothing less than an attack upon the very notion of lawmaking itself.[28]

The decision of the Court, while a personal victory for Cohen as well as for women and teachers, was less than a total victory since the Court did not decide the case on equal protection grounds. As a result, sex discriminatory policies and practices would continue to be treated differently by law and tolerated to a higher degree than would policies that discriminated on the basis of race. Subsequent decisions by the Supreme Court also showed the timidity of the Court in elevating sex discrimination to the same level as race discrimination. In this case, since another basis for legal decision was available, the Court could shy away from the equal protection issue while still striking down the discriminatory policy.

Susan Cohen was called and told of the Court decision by a friend who heard of it on the radio. She was thrilled but was less interested in the basis for the decision than her personal victory. She felt vindicated to her old school board. She was also happy to have won for professional reasons: In the years between leaving Midlothian High School and the Court decision, she had held a series of part-time jobs substituting in the local high school (often to replace pregnant teachers) and teaching in community colleges—jobs that she fit in between raising the two children she had by then. However, her once excellent teaching record in Chesterfield County (attested to by her principal at the district court hearing) was apparently in doubt after she brought suit. Cohen discovered that her teaching rating was changed after she left the school system, and the recommendation that her principal submitted for her at a new job (a letter from him was mandatory) did not reflect her original ratings.

Impact of the Supreme Court's Ruling

The impact of the Supreme Court's decision in Cohen's and La Fleur's cases on school district maternity leave policies was far reaching: Tens of thousands of women teachers could no longer legally be required to leave their jobs when they became pregnant. However, the actual impact of Cohen's case was lessened by decisions in other maternity court cases and by federal regulations. Shortly, after the Cohen decision, the Supreme Court ruled that state disability insurance need not treat pregnancy as it does all other temporary disabilities, thereby excluding pregnancy from coverage.[29] This represented a major set-back for women's rights advocates who were trying to have pregnancy accepted as a temporary disability for all reasons, including disability and health insurance and leave purposes.

In December 1976, the Supreme Court decided another important maternity disability leave case.[30] This case, which was based on the policy of the General Electric Company, unlike Cohen's case, involved the validity of the EEOC maternity leave guidelines. By a clear majority the Court rejected the argument that treating maternity different than other disabilities constituted sex discrimination. The failure of the Supreme Court to uphold EEOC guidelines on this issue was a major blow to women's rights.

While the Supreme Court's actions will have impact nationwide in all employment areas, the maternity leave policies of schools and colleges are being regulated by the Department of Health, Education and Welfare. DHEW, in its regulation implementing the Title IX anti-sex discrimination law passed by Congress in 1972, mandated that maternity leave be treated the same as all other temporary disabilities. Since the DHEW regulation is more liberal than the Court's decision in Cohen's case in prohibiting sex discrimination in maternity leave policies, for all practical purposes the maternity leave policies in all educational institutions will no longer be influenced by the Supreme Court's decision.

Actual compliance of schools with the Supreme Court's decision (before the Title IX regulation went into effect) have been difficult to assess. A study of the nation's largest school systems found that all were complying with the Court's decision.[31] The financial fear of losing lawsuits and being required by the courts to pay back salaries to women teachers (as well as having already paid for substitute replacement teachers) seems to be working as a strong incentive for schools to comply with the Court's decision. However, many schools' policies are clearly not in accordance with the broader EEOC guidelines or DHEW's regulation on maternity leave.[32] Discrimination against women for becoming pregnant continues as widespread public policy in schools. Therefore, Cohen's case, while helping to establish the legal basis for rational maternity leave policies, marks only the beginning of the legal, political, and administrative efforts that will be necessary before all elements of sex bias are removed from the way working women are treated when they become pregnant.

Concluding Observations

As this case illustrates, victories for the rights of women can derive from unexpected sources. In this particular case, a woman teacher with little interest in the women's rights movement and young lawyer with no experience in federal court joined forces to initiate a lawsuit that would eventually overturn major portions of the maternity leave policy in almost every school district in the country. However, the process involved in gaining this victory was extremely lengthy and expensive, and the Court ruling achieved was narrower in impact than had been hoped for or expected. Cohen's case illustrates how even a clear and blatantly discriminatory practice still requires an inordinate amount of effort to overturn. Part of the explanation for this lies in the intransigence of the local school officials, and part results from the nature of the judicial process itself.

One cannot help but be struck by the lack of rational decision making on the part of the school board in this case. Requiring a teacher to go on leave a few days before the end of a crucial semester for her students does not make sense from any educational or social policy perspective. The cavalier attitude with which the decision was treated made a mockery of the entire local educational decision-making process. The stubbornness displayed by the board in its decision to fight for its policy through the federal court system, at great expense to the taxpayers of the district, does little to enhance the reputation of local education agencies as intelligent policymakers.

As outrageous as the school board's actions were, they would be understandable if there was great community interest in the issue and great community support for the local policy, as there has been on other local school policies that have been challenged in court, such as prayer in the schools.

However, this was markedly not the case. Quite to the contrary, the community's reaction was generally one of apathy: There was no pressure at all placed on the school board to pursue the issue into the courts. The school board's actions seem to have been in response to an intractable role taken up voluntarily by the board members as protectors of the social order against harmful trends in regard to the role of women in American society.

The requirement of a mandatory maternity leave was an expression of male policymakers' support of the societal norm that women should work only before they have children or after their children are grown, as shown by board members' own statements. The underlying assumption of maternity policies is that a woman's major role in life should be that of a housewife and mother. This view obviously conflicted with the basic tenets of the women's rights movement. Therefore, it is not surprising that the conflict over maternity policies took on symbolic importance for the school board members who were defending them and for the women and education groups that aided Susan Cohen and Jo Carol La Fleur in challenging them. To the male board members, maternity leave was a policy that represented both the institution of the family and also their right to make unilateral, unquestioned policy decisions. To the women and education groups, maternity leave was a highly visible expression of the restrictive societal roles that had subjugated women for years and a policy that was formulated without the participation of women.

Although the decision in Cohen's case was a victory for the rights of women and of teachers, the basis for the ruling indicates that the courts are inclined to give school boards wide discretion in setting school policy, as long as the policies are aimed at and actually achieve legitimate state interests, even though this may come at the expense of the rights of women. In addition, it would seem that the courts need less justification for ruling that a sex-based policy is in the state's legitimate interest than it would need in ruling that a racially based policy is in the state's legitimate interest. For this reason, combined with the knowledge that the views of society held by young women are not the same as the views held by the older men who are judges, it must be acknowledged that relief from sex discrimination will not always result from the filing of court cases. Instead, other sources such as federal, state, and local administrative agencies, legislative bodies, and local school boards will have to be persuaded that sex discrimination is wrong and should not be tolerated before all elements of sex bias are removed from public policy.

Notes

Except where otherwise footnoted, the information presented in this chapter was obtained from interviews with the persons listed below and from documents provided by them. Also indicated is the capacity in which these people were interviewed. Of necessity, the material presented in the chapter relies on the authors' interpretation of the information obtained from these sources.

Interview with Susan E. Cohen, Teacher, January 1976.

Interview with John Bertram Mann, Attorney, April 1976.

Interview with Philip J. Hirschkop, Attorney, April 1976.

Interview with Catherine East, former Executive Secretary, Citizens' Advisory Council on the Status of Women, May 1976.

Interview with Betty Sinowitz, NEA Du Shane Fund, March 1976.

1. Susan Cohen, letter to the NEA Du Shane Fund.

2. For a full discussion of the content of these policies see: Janice Pottker and Andrew Fishel, "Sex Discrimination As Public Policy: Maternity Leave Policies for Teachers," *Educational Forum* 39 (November 1974), pp. 7-15.

3. Plaintiff Exhibit in Appendix, *Cohen* v. *Chesterfield County School Board*, 474 F. 2d 395 (4 Cir. 1973).

4. Susan Cohen, letter to NEA.

5. Deposition of Clarence E. Curtis, Jr., in Appendix, *Cohen* v. *Chesterfield County School Board*, 474 F. 2d 395 (4 Cir. 1973).

6. Deposition of C.C. Wells, ibid.

7. For the full text of the proceedings and the testimonies discussed in this section, see transcript of Court Proceedings, *Cohen* v. *Chesterfield County School Board*, 326 F. Supp. 1159 (E.D. Va. 1971).

8. Ibid.

9. Ibid.

10. "Pregnant Teacher Fights School Board," *Richmond News-Leader*, April 20, 1971.

11. Editorial, *Richmond Times Dispatch*, June 6, 1971.

12. For the full text of the arguments discussed in this section, see Brief for Appellants, *Cohen* v. *Chesterfield County School Board*, 326 F. Supp. 1159 (E.D. Va. 1971).

13. Ibid.

14. Brief for the U.S. Equal Employment Opportunity Commission as Amicus Curiae, *Cohen* v. *Chesterfield County School Board*, 474 F. 2d 395 (4 Cir. 1973).

15. Reply Brief for Appellants, ibid.

16. *Cohen* v. *Chesterfield County School Board*, No. 71-707 (4 Cir. 1972).

17. Ibid.

18. Ibid.

19. Ibid.

20. Ibid.

21. Ibid.

22. Ibid.

23. Transcript of Oral Argument, *Cleveland Board of Education* v. *La Fleur*, 94 S. Ct. 791 (1974).

24. Ibid.

25. *Cleveland Board of Education* v. *La Fleur*, 94 S. Ct. 791 (1974).

26. Ibid.

27. Ibid.

28. Ibid.

29. *Geduldig* v. *Aiello*, 417 U.S. 484 (1974).

30. John MacKenzie, "Sick Pay Ruled Not Required for Pregnant Women," *Washington Post*, December 8, 1976.

31. Janice Pottker, "Large City School Districts and Noncompliance with Federal Law: The Case of Maternity Leave Policies," Paper presented at the Annual Meeting of the American Education Research Association, Washington, D.C., 1975 (ERIC ED 108080).

32. Ibid.

3

Sex Discrimination and Bureaucratic Politics: The U.S. Office of Education's Task Force on Women's Education

Holly Knox and
Mary Ann Millsap

In November of 1972, a task force established by the U.S. Commissioner of Education, then the federal government's chief education officer, reported that DHEW's $5 billion in education aid programs were supporting widespread discrimination against girls and women throughout the nation's education system.[1] The report made thirty-three recommendations for changes in U.S. Office of Education (OE) policies and practices to discourage sex discrimination in the agency's programs.[2] This chapter chronicles the creation and activities of the Commissioner's Task Force on the Impact of Office of Education Programs on Women and the extent of implementation of its recommendations.

Background

The creation of a women's education task force in OE had its genesis in a report prepared in January 1972 by DHEW's Women's Action Program (WAP).[3] WAP had been established by DHEW Secretary, Elliot Richardson, early in 1971 to identify discrimination against women both as employees of the Department and as potential clients for its health, education, and welfare programs and to recommend changes to end that discrimination. One of the first actions of WAP was the preparation of a comprehensive report on the Department's treatment of women, combined with a series of recommendations on how all parts of DHEW could improve their services to women.

The Women's Action Program report asked the Office of Education to act to improve the status of women in vocational and higher education. Some of WAP's suggestions for OE were general; others were specific about particular program changes that were needed. Richardson moved quickly to encourage adoption of the report's recommendations throughout the Department. On January 18, days after the report was released, he sent a memorandum to all DHEW top officials asking them to report back on "a plan of specific steps, and a timetable . . . whereby your agency or office will take action to carry out the recommendation or otherwise undertake to achieve its objectives." According to the memorandum, if officials disagreed with a recommendation, they should explain why and submit a plan for alternative means of achieving the same aim; the Secretary also encouraged his agency heads to go beyond the recommendations and asked that plans be sent to his office within a month.

The Commissioner Establishes a Task Force

Ultimately, the Commissioner of Education's response to this mandate from Secretary Richardson was the creation in May 1972 of a twelve-person task force to take a broader look at the problems of sex discrimination in OE's more than one hundred education programs.

Commissioner Sidney P. Marland's decision to set up this study group of OE employees came in the wake of a series of events, both inside and outside the agency. Congress was then moving toward the enactment of a sweeping new law barring federal aid to education programs that discriminated on the basis of sex—Title IX of the Education Amendments of 1972. Public concern about sex discrimination was rising, and congressional hearings held by Republican Edith Green (D., Ore.) had spotlighted evidence of extensive sex bias in education, particularly in graduate school admissions and in tenured and administrative positions.[4]

Before the creation of the Task Force, the response from within the Office of Education to Secretary Richardson's mandate for change was lackadaisical. By late March, only two OE top officials even answered the memorandum the commissioner's office sent out in mid-February asking for plans to implement the Women's Action Program recommendations.

Charged with preparing OE's response to Secretary Richardson's mandate, the Federal Women's Program Coordinator began to urge the Commissioner to set up a task force to document what the Office of Education had done to improve the status of women in American education and suggest other actions. The Women's Program Coordinator was a feminist whose responsibility—like that of her counterparts in every federal agency—was trying to improve employment opportunities for women in the agency. She saw the Secretary's request for action as a chance to document sex bias in the agency's programs and therefore used the opportunity to press for a special study of sex discrimination in education programs. Previously, OE had created a similar group to examine sex bias in its own employment practices; however, that group had not analyzed OE's programs from the perspective of equity for the sexes.

In May of 1972, Commissioner Marland created a temporary task force. It appears that the task force idea was accepted by Marland because OE's response up until that time to the Secretary's request for action had been inadequate and because the Women's Action Program report itself did not offer a broad look at sex discrimination in the agency's programs. While the Office of Education administered over one hundred separate aid "programs" supporting all aspects of education—from preschool to adult literacy education, from instructional equipment to libraries to research—the Women's Action Program report had touched only on vocational, graduate, and adult education.

Within DHEW in the early 1970s, internal task forces were a common way of exploring current policy issues and coming up with new solutions, especially if the issues cut across several organizational units. A task force usually drew staff people from different parts of the Department or agency, worked on the issue part-time, and made recommendations to top officials. Sometimes task forces served principally to sideline difficult issues; sometimes they were honest attempts to devise new policy proposals. The task force reports, with a few notable exceptions, were rarely made public.

The Commissioner's Task Force on Impact of Office of Education Programs on Women was charged to:

Examine all Office of Education programs in terms of their impact on and discrimination against women;

Identify the need for data by sex, where existing data did not offer enough information to judge a program's impact on women;

Suggest ways of implementing the Women's Action Program recommendations;

Identify other problems and recommend remedial action; and

Recommend procedures for tracking the progress of federal education programs in providing equal opportunity for both sexes.

The group was not to investigate sex bias in the agency's own employment practices, since a study of this issue had already been made. From the outset, the Task Force had an extremely broad mandate: to suggest ways of putting the Women's Action Program recommendations into practice, to assess the impact on women and possible sex discrimination in every Office of Education program, and to recommend remedies and procedures for seeing that they were carried out. Like most task forces, the group was created only to do a report; once its mission was finished, it would be dissolved.

Education Officials Appoint Task Force Members

While Commissioner Marland's early May memo outlined the basic structure of the Task Force, the Commissioner left the appointment of its members to his deputy commissioners. These men were, in effect, the "commissioner's cabinet" of senior officials; each was responsible either for a number of aid programs in a broad area of education, such as higher education, vocational education, or for legislation, public relations, or planning/management. Each of the deputy commissioners was asked to appoint staff members to the Task Force. No qualifications were stipulated, except that the Commissioner encouraged the appointment of men as well as women. The Commissioner asked that the members be freed from their regular work one day a week for eight weeks; the group was to report its findings and recommendations at the end of two months.

Few of the Task Force members who were selected knew why or how they had been chosen; in fact, many came to the first meeting in complete ignorance of the nature of the group to which they had been appointed. A small number—perhaps three of those originally chosen—had been active as advocates of equality for women before. Most, however, had no background of feminist activity, and a few of the original appointees appeared to be so unsympathetic to the group's aim that they removed themselves. The study group, when it finally assembled in mid-May, consisted of nine women and three men.

The Activities of the Task Force

The Task Force met for the first time in mid-May of 1972. While the Federal Women's Program Coordinator and the chairperson had a fairly clear idea of what they wanted the Task Force to accomplish, no one really knew how to collect the necessary information or how to deal with a loosely connected OE bureaucracy of some two thousand employees. In fact, only two Task Force members had a broad knowledge of OE programs; most of the others worked in relatively autonomous units and had had little contact with other programs.

One of the first conclusions reached by the group was that more than eight working days (one day a week for eight weeks) would be needed to do a credible job of assessing sex discrimination in education and making recommendations for action that OE could not ignore through common bureaucratic tactics. Two Task Force members began to reorganize their other work to devote nearly full-time to this effort.[a]

The initial activities of the Task Force were of two types: informing all OE staff of the creation of the task force in order to facilitate initial data collection and exploring their own feelings and attitudes toward sex discrimination. A memorandum was sent to all OE staff describing the creation of the Task Force and its mission and requesting their support. During the first month of activity, questionnaires tailored to OE's hundred-plus programs were developed. The questions were far ranging; for example: How many persons by sex are enrolled in each type or level of program? What are the stipends for men and women (in financial aid programs)? What proportion of project directors (administrators) are women? Are efforts being made to insure all persons have equal access to the programs? Are there any special projects aimed at expanding opportunities for women?

The questionnaires were sent to each program. Within three days of their receipt, Task Force members were to meet with program administrators to help

[a]That Task Force members were allowed to reorganize work suggests silent approval by parts of the bureaucracy for activities of the Task Force. In both cases, the Task Force members were told by their supervisors that they could spend as much time as they wanted on the Task Force, provided that their regular work was completed on schedule.

them with their questions. Cooperation was largely passive; there was little active support or active resistance to Task Force activities. Most program administrators did cooperate, probably because the Task Force had the nominal support of the Commissioner, internal employment practices (a more sensitive issue) were explicitly not included in the Task Force mandate, and program files were normally open to other OE employees who had the patience to examine them.

When the data were first tallied in June, the Task Force realized that while sex bias clearly existed in many OE programs, OE had very little information on the sex of the persons that it served; on how many field administrators were women; or on the efforts, if any, to reduce sex bias in programs or materials. Although sex discrimination was evident in restrictive course offerings and stipends in vocational and higher education (the area of concentration in the Women's Action Program Report), sex bias was also evident in curriculum and guidance materials, research studies, and OE-sponsored questionnaires. Much of this information was gleaned not from program questionnaires, but from reports, program files, and reviews of the research in the area.

Task Force members discovered early on that few program administrators were aware of what sex discrimination meant. On more than one occasion, Task Force members were told: "I don't know why you're concerned with this program; we don't teach sex education."

Once the initial data were in and Task Force members realized the lack of data and lack of awareness about sex discrimination, the Task Force began a review of available literature and program documents to ascertain the current status of women in education. At the same time, a much-needed time extension was obtained on the due date for the Task Force report.

Group meetings were held at least weekly to discuss findings to date, possible recommendations for OE action, and ways of organizing what had become, in the Task Force members' minds, a large comprehensive document. Criteria were set up by the Task Force to examine each proposed recommendation in terms of its significance, likelihood of adoption, practicality of implementation, and numbers of persons affected. For any recommendation to be included, it had to be agreed upon by voice vote by a majority of Task Force members.

While debate on recommendations often took center stage during the group meetings, organizing the report was the Task Force's major work. The Task Force members decided that it was vital that the report provide a comprehensive review of sexism in education (since few OE officials were aware of the problem); that each reference be checked and rechecked so that the report would be beyond criticism on factual grounds; and that the report clearly specify not only each recommendation but also the administrative unit in DHEW responsible for implementing it.

These needs developed out of perceptions Task Force members had of the OE bureaucracy. The initial data collection indicated that OE staff not only were ignorant of what sex discrimination meant but also did not perceive its existence in their programs. In addition, the Task Force felt that many officials would be reluctant to change their policies and would either fasten on procedural excuses for not changing (e.g., coordination too difficult or it wasn't clear who was in charge) or would seek out information in the report they could discredit, casting doubt on the entire report and its recommendations. The net result would be the same: no action.

In its report, following the overview chapter on sex discrimination in education, the Task Force grouped its recommendations into two chapters: (a) "The Legal Imperative," which included the necessary steps to carry out Title IX and Executive Order 11246 to end discrimination in federal education programs, and (b) "Beyond the Legal Imperative," which included a plan for creative federal leadership in fulfilling the spirit of the laws against sex discrimination. An appendix to the report presented a listing of each OE and NIE unit and the recommendations associated with it.

The chapter on "The Legal Imperative" outlined the major areas of sex bias directly supported by federal education funds, the actions already taken by a few OE offices to counteract sex discrimination in programs they administer, the steps the Assistant Secretary for Education and the agency heads reporting to the Assistant Secretary must take to live up to basic legal requirements, and the steps the Office for Civil Rights should take to strengthen enforcement procedures. The recommendations to OE and NIE[b] included, for example:

Making the legal obligations to eliminate sex discrimination under Title IX and Executive Order 11246 known to all potential and actual recipients of federal education aid;

Providing information and technical assistance on Title IX to state and local educational personnel;

Insuring that all instructional and public relations materials developed with OE and NIE funds for national distribution be free of sex biases;

Having OE and NIE work together to eliminate sex discrimination in career preparation;

Working to equalize the proportion of men and women at all levels and in all areas of education through training programs and promoting the involvement of women in top positions in OE- and NIE-funded projects.

The chapter entitled "Beyond the Legal Imperative" outlined the most important roles DHEW's education units should play in educating the public, helping students and teachers to explore new roles for both sexes, fostering new

---

[b]NIE is the research and development branch of the Education Division and was created during the preparation of the Task Force report.

educational approaches, and knowledge building. Finally, it listed the internal management changes the education agencies ought to make if they were serious in their commitment of championing women's right to equal educational opportunities over the long term. Recommendations in this chapter were very diverse and ranged from provisions for child care and part-time study; changes in OE surveys to collect and report data by sex; educating the public to setting equality for the sexes in education as an official priority in OE and NIE; educating OE and NIE staff to avoid sex bias in agency operation and program management; and to the establishment in OE and NIE of a Women's Action Office.

In October of 1972, meetings were held with a few OE officials to elicit their reactions to the recommendations. In November, the completed 140-page Task Force report was submitted to the Commissioner of Education. With the submission of its report, the Task Force was formally disbanded.

First Reactions to the Report

By the time the task force submitted its final report in November 1972, Sidney Marland, who had commissioned it, had moved "upstairs" to a new position as Assistant Secretary for Education. However, initial reactions to the report from Marland's successor, Commissioner John Ottina, were supportive, and it appeared that the group's recommendations might be off to a good start.

Meeting with Task Force representatives shortly after the report was finished, Ottina praised the report.[c] Management-oriented, Ottina particularly praised the report's breakdown of exactly which agency units would have to act on each recommendation. This format would save his staff a great deal of work, and it made acting on the Task Force's suggestions much more feasible.

At that meeting, the Task Force delegation reported to Ottina the Task Force's own priorities among the thirty-three recommendations. The Task Force representatives also stressed the group's belief that it was vital that action on its recommendations be tracked through the agency's Operational Planning System (OPS). This system, which had been introduced throughout DHEW several years before as a way to increase accountability fo. bureaucratic accomplishments, required top officials to state their most important objectives and map out concrete steps with specific dates for their completion. Since these officials had to report in person to the Commissioner each month on their progress, they would have to account regularly for any failures to meet program commitments. Although the system had weaknesses, it was sometimes a powerful lever for

[c]Commissioner Ottina was not the only official who appeared supportive. Secretary Richardson, to whom the report was sent simply for his information, jotted a handwritten note to the (new) Assistant Secretary Marland: "Very impressive. Congratulations. I trust that this will be followed up."

forcing action in a bureaucracy so large and inefficient that commitments were routinely simply not acted upon.

The Task Force stressed the importance of using the OPS system for tracking progress on equity for women for several reasons. The inclusion of goals aimed at achieving women's equity in the Operational Planning System would in itself have represented a commitment at the top of the agency, since only the objectives deemed most important by the Commissioner, or the Secretary, were included in the OPS system. In addition, implementing the recommendations required action by so many bureaucratic units that it would be impossible for anyone to know what was happening without the formal reporting structure imposed by OPS. Finally, the Task Force expected resistance to the mandate for changes to promote equal opportunity for women and felt that unless program administrators were held accountable by the Commissioner himself for progress, most would do nothing.

While Ottina made no commitments to Task Force representatives to adopt recommendations during the December meeting, he did make some promises concerning the report's distribution. Besides distributing it to education officials in charge of programs, Ottina agreed to:

Make the full report available to anyone who asked for it;

Send out a press release on the report;

Have the public affairs office edit and publish the report for a general audience, so that the agency could do a mailing to a broad spectrum of the education community (Task Force members agreed the full report was too lengthy and technical for a broad audience).

Task Force members felt Ottina's agreement to publicize the report was important since internal task force reports were usually not released to the public. Task Force members felt publicity for the report was important to help inform educators—most of whom appeared to be unaware of the injustices caused by sex discrimination in education—about the problems girls and women face. Moreover, Task Force members who were pessimistic about the likelihood that agency officials would readily agree to implement the recommendations believed that public pressure—public embarrassment, if necessary—was essential to secure more than the most token changes. And public pressure would be impossible if the report were not released.

Ottina's decision to release the report may have been influenced by a memorandum he received from Richardson shortly before the report was completed. Congratulating the Office of Education for appointing the Task Force, Richardson said:

I think the task force report should have the widest possible circulation within the Department and among selected outside groups. This will enable the

Department to create a momentum for change that will set an example for other government agencies.

Ottina's commitment to distribute and publicize the report gave the Task Force members hope that their report might have an impact both inside the agency and out. Despite these commitments, though, the report was handled in a way that kept public exposure to a minimum. Ultimately, the report was mailed out only to people who found out about it and wrote in asking for it. Ottina rejected a proposal from the Public Affairs Office that it be sent initially to a list of key women's group leaders and members of Congress. The edited version for mass circulation was never completed.

Finally, the press release, drafted by a public affairs office that was unused to and undoubtedly uncomfortable with writing a release on a report critical of the agency, was so bland that it discouraged press interest. In the end, only two newspaper articles on the report appeared.

Many people already concerned about equity for women in education, both in Washington and around the country, did hear about the report—by word of mouth, through women's groups, newsletters, or through its eventual publication in the Senate hearings on the Women's Educational Equity Act.[5] But the Office of Education's failure to fulfill its commitment to publicize the report and disseminate it widely meant that those who might have had the most to learn from the report—educators still unaware of the problem of sexism in their own institutions—never heard of it. Just as important, the report never drew the public attention that might have helped pressure the agency to carry out its recommendations.

The Office of Education Devises a Plan
to Carry Out the Changes

The Office of Education took nine months to complete its formal response to the Task Force's recommendations. That agency officials responded on paper at all is worth noting, as this was by no means common practice for task force reports.

The process was set in motion by a memorandum, from Ottina to his deputy commissioners. He asked each deputy commissioner for an implementation plan by February 16. The date was one year past the deadline Secretary Richardson had originally placed on the submission of plans to implement the Women's Action Program recommendations. The Commissioner turned over responsibility for coordinating these plans to the Office for Special Concerns, the office that had previously pressed for creation of the Task Force and had been responsible to the Commissioner for its progress. Over the next few months, the Office for Special Concerns staff devoted considerable time and energy to these plans: pressing Deputy Commissioners' staff people to work on the plans, reviewing and critiquing them, and nudging and prodding. By late spring, all but one of the deputy commissioners had submitted revised plans. An order from his superior, the Commissioner of Education, could have forced the single recalcitrant Deputy Commissioner to submit a plan, but such an order was never issued.

In June of 1973, the Commissioner of Education approved a final implementation plan for the Task Force recommendations. The 72-page plan, composed mainly of the plans from each deputy commissioner with some additional action steps proposed by the Office for Special Concerns, was eventually forwarded to the Secretary for his information and returned to the deputy commissioners with instructions to carry out the plans.

The plan did commit the Office of Education to undertake some important actions. The Commissioner agreed to establish a women's program office. "Among other duties," the plan indicated "this office will monitor the implementation of this Task Force report."

In addition, OE committed itself to:

Distribute detailed information on Title IX to all fund applicants "immediately" after the regulation took effect;

Train all OE program directors in civil rights requirements;

Develop checklists to allow Office of Education program staff to include Title IX compliance checks in all regular site reviews;

Develop guidelines for avoiding sex bias in materials developed with agency funds;

Review materials developed with agency funds for sex bias;

Include a standard paragraph in appropriate guidelines, requests for proposals, and so forth, stating that as a condition for funding, applicants would have to develop materials which are free of sex and racial stereotyping;

Compile a list of women's organizations and place them on program mailing lists to encourage women to apply for agency funds;

Prepare a guide for avoiding sex bias in research questionnaires;

Collect more data broken down by sex both on its programs and on the educational system generally;

Publish summaries of agency-funded projects aimed at improving educational opportunities for girls and women;

Publish an annual summary of data available on women in education;

Send a memorandum to the Secretary urging him to increase the percentage of women on each advisory council to 50 percent of the total.

On the whole, the implementation plan was a rather bewildering mixture of serious commitments, recitations of actions already initiated, and rationales for not implementing particular recommendations. In addition, the plan contained many vague, confusing, and irrelevant commitments. For example, the Deputy Commissioner for Occupational and Adult Education responded to the recommendation to increase the number of women in fields currently dominated by men with a promise to employ a guidance specialist; he also answered the recommendation that the agency develop guidance materials specifically designed to overcome sex stereotyping with the somewhat mysterious notation that "the National Guidance Handbook on Vocational Education Programs will be ready."

Agency officials rejected several recommendations outright, but generally very few recommendations were openly rejected. This response conformed to the general bureaucratic tendency in OE toward passive resistance. OE administrators generally find it easier to say "yes," or "maybe," or "we'll study it," or answer with an undecipherable cloud of verbiage—and not act—than to openly reject a suggested course of action. A simple "no" offered a clear target for opposition; the other alternatives were much more difficult to criticize.

Promises, Promises—What Really Happened

Flawed as it was, the 1973 implementation plan did represent some explicit commitments by the Commissioner of Education and his top officials to take steps to reduce the agency's support for sex discrimination in education. By the spring of 1976 no precise accounting of which of these commitments had been fulfilled was available since the agency never followed through on the suggestion to track progress through the Operational Planning System. However, available evidence suggests that while several of the commitments were carried out, many were simply forgotten.

Shortly after the implementation plan was approved, the Office for Special Concerns focused its energy on seeing that one key recommendation—the creation of a women's action office—was carried out. After considerable bureaucratic infighting, a small office labeled the "Women's Program Staff" was created in January 1974, with an acting director and a secretary. The new women's office was relatively dormant until a permanent director was appointed in May 1974. By the time the fledgling unit was created, the Office for Special Concerns had itself been dissolved, thereby eliminating that office as a source of internal pressure for implementing the Task Force recommendations.

Between June 1973, when the 72-page implementation plan was approved, and May 1974, when a permanent director for the new Women's Program Staff was hired, little action on the recommendations appears to have taken place. During that period, Congress was moving toward passage of the "Women's Educational Equity Act," a bill to provide funds—through the Office of

Education—to projects designed to improve opportunities for girls and women in education. The bill eventually became law in August 1974. During Senate hearings on the bill, the 1972 Task Force report was frequently cited as evidence for the need for the bill.[6] Administration witnesses, however, opposed the bill and argued that funds for projects promoting equal educational opportunity for women could come from existing Office of Education programs.

Following closely on the heels of DHEW's testimony opposing the "Women's Educational Equity Act," the bill's Senate sponsor, Walter F. Mondale (D., Minn.), requested that DHEW report on the Office of Education's progress in implementing Task Force recommendations to support equality of the sexes.[7] The report on most recommendations was one of no action to date (one year after the task force submitted its report).

Shortly after the Director of the new Women's Program Staff was appointed the following May, she made an attempt to find out which of the plans to implement the Task Force's recommendations had been carried out. In June 1974 she sent a memorandum to all top officials asking for a report of progress on their own implementation plans. By the end of August, only five out of ten OE offices had reported back fully. In those reports that did come in, many of the action steps were reported as deleted, uninitiated, not completed, or in progress: There were few concrete results. For the most part, no reasons for "deleting" previous commitments or failing to carry them out were offered.

Since May 1974, the Women's Program Staff and a few other OE offices have made concerted efforts to carry out a number of the responsibilities assigned to them as a result of the Task Force report.[8] For example, in-staff training programs to increase sensitivity to sex bias were organized, and the elimination of sex-stereotyping in vocational education was made a major program objective. Alongside these activities, however, were numerous set-backs for implementation of the recommendations. The women's office was unable to press for or achieve progress in many of the areas where the Task Force advised that changes should be made. A major reason for not doing so was that a substantial portion of the office's energies were devoted to the task of administering the Women's Education Equity Act. The Women's Program office was working on plans to administer the Act from the time the Act was passed in August 1974. Chronically understaffed, the office had to pick its priorities carefully.

In addition, the office had an extremely difficult time even getting formal reports from program administrators on their progress in implementing Task Force recommendations or responding to its own action requests. The June 1974 memorandum asking for a comprehensive report was not the only one that drew little response. As a result, in September 1974, Duane Matheis, the Executive Deputy Commissioner to whom the Women's Program office reports, sent an unusually acerbic memorandum to his fellow deputy commissioners. He listed five separate requests for information sent in June and July by the

Women's Program Staff and noted which units had failed to respond to each request. Out of ten units, half had ignored a request to name a contact person on sex-bias problems, a request for a listing of exemplary projects for overcoming sex bias, a status report on progress on its plan for carrying out the task force recommendations, and a survey on data collection. "The response," Matheis noted in the memo, "has not been universally excellent.... The increased activity and responsibility assigned to the Women's Program Office mandates our complete support in their efforts. . . ."

Assessment of the Office of Education's Response

In the end, the Office of Education did openly reject a few of the Task Force recommendations. For example, the agency did refuse to accept the recommendation that all relevant programs should collect data on their beneficiaries by sex, despite the significance of this information. In addition, some important recommendations were lost when the official agency plan omitted them. Others, which were difficult to implement, simply were never pursued.

Of the commitments for action the agency did make, some were fulfilled, but many, it seems, were simply forgotten. As of April 1976, actions still unfulfilled included:

Publishing and disseminating a scaled down version of the report for consumption by the education community;

Developing guidelines for avoiding sex bias for use by agency staff and contractors who are developing materials;

Drafting checklists so that agency staff can include a brief Title IX compliance check in regular visits to projects they've funded;

Drafting a standard paragraph for all appropriate guidelines stating that as a condition of funding applicants for material development funds would have to avoid sex and race bias;

Preparing a guide for avoiding sex bias in research questionnaires.

The Office of Education's failure to fulfill many of its own promises undoubtedly had many causes. The Office of Education is a bureaucracy whose inertia and resistance to change has confounded administrators and political leaders for years. Real change in the way the Office of Education views and responds to the issue of sex bias in education would have required numerous conditions that either did not exist or existed inadequately. For change to have been accomplished, the following would have been necessary:

1. Outside pressure from forces in the society to which the political

leadership must respond. There was limited interest and little pressure from groups outside DHEW for implementation of the Task Force report.

2. Strong, persistent, and visible commitment at the top. Secretary Richardson appears to have been committed to tackling sex bias in DHEW's programs, but he left DHEW soon after the OE Task Force made its report. There is no evidence that Commissioner Ottina made supporting equity for women a personal priority, and he does not seem to have seriously pressed his top administrators for action. With one or two exceptions, these administrators appear to have largely ignored the report and their own plans to respond to it.

3. A system of holding administrators accountable for action or inaction. Agency officials made only limited use of the tools they had for keeping track of progress in matters of prime importance to the leadership. The Operational Planning System, the only practical means at hand for checking on the implementation of the complex recommendations, was used through 1976 only to track two projects undertaken by the Women's Program Staff. These were the training program for agency personnel and the activities of the Task Force exploring the need for more data by sex.

4. The presence of skillful and strategically situated internal advocates. To a certain extent the Women's Program staff met this criterion, although whether its position in the hierarchy was "strategic" is open to debate. While the office boasted impressive accomplishments for its size, it has always been drastically understaffed. In addition, as of summer 1976, the office had won little visible personal support from the agency's top administrator, the Commissioner of Education.

The Task Force itself, of course, was disbanded after reporting and could not function as a pressure group working for implementation. Individual members did press within their own bureaucratic units for action, but none exerted serious pressure for action agencywide.

NIE's Response to the Task Force Report

The National Institute of Education (NIE), the research and development arm of the Education Division, was created during the writing of the Task Force report. Since most of NIE's early programs were inherited from OE, the Task Force included NIE in its report and recommendations.

In December of 1972, the Assistant Secretary for Education transmitted the Task Force report to NIE's Director for action. Upon receipt of the report, the Director asked one of the senior women in the Institute (and an active feminist) to set up an ad hoc committee to react to the recommendations.

The committee reacted to the appropriateness of the recommendations and noted which units should be responsible for implementing them. It did not, however, establish detailed procedures or timelines for implementation in its

May 1973 report to the Director, and the Director never asked for such a plan. To its credit, the committee did circulate its report widely within the Institute and urged the Institute to broaden employment policies such as the hiring of men and women desiring part-time work.

The uniqueness of NIE as a new and rather small agency of some 350 employees both helped and hindered the implementation of Task Force recommendations. On the plus side, women concerned about sex discrimination were appointed to two of the six associate director—"director's cabinet"—positions, with authority over program budgets (as heads of the Education and Work Group and the Dissemination and Resources Group); men and women were permitted to work part-time; programs were funded with a focus on women; and funds were set aside for a separate Women's Research Program in the Educational Equity Group.

At the same time, NIE has had a rocky existence from its inception. The Institute was created as a consequence of a presidential initiative, midst great expectations to be different and better than OE's research and development program. Initial appropriations only covered support for the transferred OE programs. It was assumed that appropriations would remain at this level, thereby giving NIE flexibility to fund new programs as OE programs terminated. NIE's enabling legislation mandated that its policies toward educational research and development be set by an external policy board—the National Council on Educational Research. Delays in the appointment and confirmation of the fifteen Council members created problems with Congress and resulted in severe cuts in NIE's requested appropriation. In addition, Congress was apparently not convinced of NIE's utility; a debate about whether the Institute would continue to exist started fairly early on. Because of these factors, the Institute has been more concerned with survival than with long-range planning, and the attention given to women's issues has suffered as a result.

Still, NIE did have several management mechanisms available to it, including the Operational Planning System, which it could have used to keep track of the progress being made on objectives relating to women's education. However, it did not use the OPS or any other mechanism to monitor the implementation of the Task Force recommendations. The Federal Women's Program Coordination position, the position most likely to press for implementation, was not filled until fourteen months after the Task Force report was transmitted to the Director for action. As of the spring of 1976, the Women's Program Coordinator was working more than half-time on other duties and the time she devoted to women's issues was spent more on improving employment opportunities for women in the Institute than with the effects of NIE programs on women.

Within its organizational work groups, NIE took positive steps toward implementing several of the Task Force recommendations, particularly those related to career education. The Education and Work Group made the concerns of eliminating sex discrimination in education an integral part of much of its program, including funding such projects as:

Development of guidelines for the assessment of sex bias and sex fairness in career interest inventories, conduct of workshops, and preparation of a book entitled, *Issues of Sex Bias and Sex Fairness in Career Interest Measurement;*[9]

Continuation of a multiyear OE development project to create a counseling/guidance service for adults (mostly women) at home who wish to return to school or work;[10]

Development of a learning kit for guidance counselors and counselor educators about sex fair guidance and counseling for their students;[11] and most recently

The design and multiyear development of a TV series with supporting materials and activities aimed to expand career awareness by making ethnicity and sex less significant as predictors of occupational preference.

In the Educational Equity Group the general problem addressed by the Women's Research Program has been women's underrepresentation in areas of academic and occupational achievement. In addressing the issue of educational and occupational equality of women, the Women's Research Program has focused on five major areas: educational leadership and achievement; educational and occupational problems of minority women; social, psychological, and economic factors inhibiting educational equality; the impact of the educational system on women; and factors affecting sex differences in cognition.

While these efforts were significant first steps, it should be noted that only $4.1 million of NIE's total budget of $255 million in fiscal years 1973-1975 were expended on programs targeted to women in education; with the exception of $500,000 for the Women's Research Program, these funds were expended almost entirely within one of NIE's six major units—the Education and Work Group. Although only limited flexible funds were available due to legal commitments to continue support for OE-initiated programs, NIE on the whole did not target the funds that were available on projects concerned with women's education.

Within NIE, the Task Force recommendations were primarily used as a guide and initial impetus for those persons already interested in eliminating sex discrimination in educational employment and programs. No formal procedures or timelines were ever implemented, and the Task Force recommendations addressed were carried out primarily through the efforts of individual women, serving either as program heads or as program staff.

Concluding Observations

By the spring of 1976, the Task Force, its report, and its recommendations were all but forgotten. Even the Women's Program office, which was created as a result of the Task Force, had stopped sending out copies to the few inquiries that continued to trickle in; the report was, they said, "out of print."

Some interest in the fate of the Task Force's recommendations was rekindled in mid-1976 by the Advisory Council on Women's Educational Programs. This Council, which was established by mandate of the Women's Educational Equity Act, decided to undertake its own broad review of HEW education programs and their impact on women. The Council's review began with an assessment of how much OE and NIE had accomplished in response to the Task Force's suggestions. Many of these suggestions, as indicated previously, were ultimately ignored. Where they were acted on, it was almost always because someone concerned about equity for women (usually women, but not always) pressed for action within his or her office.

At the same time, other forces besides the Task Force's work contributed to a climate within the education bureaucracy more favorable to progress on women's rights. The rise of feminism and public awareness about inequities facing females has had its influence on DHEW, and the passage of Title IX itself has created some impetus for change within the education agencies. In addition, the increase in research on sex discrimination in education that has occurred since completion of the Task Force report has undoubtedly had some influence on the federal education agencies. Today it is nearly impossible to distinguish which changes may have been precipitated by the work of the 1972 Task Force and which changes have come about independently.

In sum, few of the Task Force's specific recommendations had been carried out four years after they were made. Many of the offices in DHEW's Education Division appear virtually untouched, either by the Task Force's work or by the larger societal movement for equality of the sexes. Here and there, however, the period from 1972 to 1976 has clearly seen slow but concrete progress. Federal aid programs are now being used to improve the status of girls and women in education through such approaches as the funding of special projects, the rewriting of program guidelines and regulations, and the revising of program priorities. While the overall progress may be small, the fact that any progress has been made in the face of massive bureaucratic inertia must be considered a major accomplishment in itself.

Notes

1. The authors were both members of the Task Force, but are solely responsible for this chapter. Of necessity, the narrative style of the presentation relies on the authors' own interpretations of the events described.

2. U.S. Office of Education, *Report of the Commissioner's Task Force on the Impact of Office of Education Programs on Women* (Washington, D.C.: U.S. Office of Education, November 1972). Copies of the report (ED091957) may be ordered from the ERIC Document Reproduction Service, P.O. Box 190,

Arlington, Virginia, 22210. The cost for a paper copy is $16.97; for microfilm, the cost is $.76.

3. U.S. Department of Health, Education and Welfare, *Report of the Women's Action Program* (Washington, D.C.: DHEW, January 1972).

4. U.S. House of Representatives, *Hearings before the House Special Subcommittee on Education, Committee on Education and Labor on Discrimination Against Women*, 91st Congress, 2nd Session, Washington, D.C., 1970.

5. U.S. Senate, *Hearings before the Senate Subcommittee on Education, Committee on Labor and Public Welfare on Women's Educational Equity Act of 1973*, 93rd Congress, 1st Session, Washington, D.C., 1973, pp. 149-229.

6. Ibid.

7. Ibid.

8. For a complete listing of projects funded by OE and NIE relating to women, see U.S. Department of Health, Education and Welfare, *Focus on Women: A Guide to Programs and Research in the Education Division* (Washington, D.C.: DHEW, 1976).

9. Esther E. Diamond, Editor, *Issues of Sex Bias and Sex Fairness in Career Interest Measurement* (Washington, D.C.: National Institute of Education, 1975).

10. Education Development Center, *Final Report of the Home-Community Based Career Education Project* (Newton, Mass.: Education Development Center, 1976).

11. The Learning Kit is available from Abt Associates, 55 Wheeler Street, Cambridge, Mass. 02138.

4

Sex Discrimination and the Legislative Process: The Enactment of the Women's Educational Equity Act

Most case studies of the congressional process concern themselves with the passage of a major piece of national legislation. The subject of this case study, the Women's Educational Equity Act, clearly does not fit into this category, since it cannot be considered a major national program. This is not to say the Act is not important; as the first piece of legislation enacted by Congress that has exclusively as its aim the funding of projects to improve the quality of women's education, the law will certainly serve as a catalyst for changing and improving the type of education women receive. However, a law, which has as its main provisions establishing a council to advise the U.S. Office of Education (OE) on women's education and providing of a relatively small amount of funding for research and demonstration projects on women's education, cannot be considered of vital national significance. In all likelihood, many people in the country are not, or will never be, aware that the law was enacted (although they may see the results of its existence in their schools and colleges).

What makes the history of this law interesting is that it provides an excellent example of how a few dedicated people, supported by special interest groups and a few members of Congress, can get a relatively obscure piece of legislation considered and adopted by Congress. A more typical fate for such legislation would be for it to die after being introduced and referred to a committee.[a] The case of the Women's Educational Equity Act also illustrates how a small bill gets caught up in larger political issues and has its fate affected by these issues.

What makes the history of the bill important is that it represents one of the first successful attempts on the part of women groups to use the congressional process to achieve a legislative objective that benefited their own special concern, in the same way as so many other special interest groups have used the legislative process to gain benefits for their particular constituencies. The activities of women's groups and sympathetic education groups on behalf of the Women's Educational Equity Act clearly demonstrated that these groups could be an influential force in the congressional process on issues of concern to women.

Development of the Legislative Proposal

In the fall of 1971 Arlene Horowitz, a college-educated and politically concerned woman, was working in a clerical capacity for the House of Representa-

---

[a]Only around 10 percent of bills and resolutions introduced in Congress are ever reported out of the committee to which they are referred.

tives Education and Labor Committee. In the course of her job, she was exposed to numerous education bills aimed at special and narrow fields, such as drug abuse education, ethnic studies, and environmental studies. Personally frustrated with a job she considered as making inadequate use of her education and political experience, Horowitz, like so many other women at the time, began thinking about the sex-role stereotyping that results in women being placed in these inferior positions. Attendance at various seminars and meetings where women's role in society was discussed started her thinking about a bill that would help support women's studies activities that were beginning to become popular at colleges and universities around the country. In the hope of finding support and assistance for the development of such a legislative proposal, she contacted Dr. Bernice Sandler who was at the time one of the leaders of the Women's Equity Action League (WEAL), a national women's rights organization. Sandler was skeptical about the chance of such a bill actually being passed, but was supportive of the idea of developing a bill and suggested other women who might be willing to work on developing the proposal.

Eventually, a group of seven women joined together to work on the initial conceptualization and writing of the bill. The group's members were highly experienced in and committed to the women's rights movement. The members also brought to the project job experience with a wide variety of governmental and private organizations. However, none of the women had practice in drafting legislation or extensive backgrounds in working on legislative proposals. In addition to Horowitz and Sandler, the initial group was composed of representatives from the American Association of University Women, the Department of Labor's Women's Bureau, the Interstate Association of Commissions on the Status of Women, the General Service Administration's Equal Employment Opportunity Office, and the National Women's Political Caucus. Eventually, this group would expand to include other women who were working in the women's rights area.

Working under the aegis of WEAL and calling their undertaking the Project on Equality in Education, these women devoted many evenings and weekends during the fall of 1971 and winter of 1972 to developing the legislative proposal. Arlene Horowitz, who had no legal training or bill-drafting experience, prepared a first rough draft of a bill for the group to consider. Drawing heavily from sections in other, similar education program bills and occasionally using verbatim language from appropriate sections in these bills, she prepared the initial draft that was presented to the WEAL group. The members of the group all agreed that much rewriting and reorganizing needed to be done before the proposed bill would be ready for introduction (an event they could not even be sure of since they had not as yet approached any members of Congress to sponsor it).

The initial drafts of the proposals were entitled "Women's Studies Act" and clearly reflected this rather narrow orientation. The draft bill's main emphasis at this point was the provision of financial support for the initiation and maintenance of women's studies programs in all levels of schooling. The initial drafts would also have established an advisory council on women's education studies, which would advise the Office of Education on aiding these women's studies programs. The proposal contained an arbitrarily set level of $10 million in 1974, $20 million in 1975, and $35 million in 1976, which was to have been authorized by Congress to be spent on the activities provided for in the bill.

After numerous discussions about the purpose and direction of the bill, the WEAL group revised the bill and retitled it the "Women's Education Act." This revised version no longer limited funding to courses in women's studies; instead, it focused on providing support for the development of materials and curricula to improve all aspects of women's education. The training of teachers and administrators so that they might become more sensitive to the current educational needs of girls and women was also provided for. The WEAL group had purposely drafted the bill so that the type of programs to be supported were numerous, diverse, and all-encompassing. Since sex discrimination was seen as existing at every level and in every aspect of the education system, the group wanted to include every possible use for which funds might be necessary in the effort to eliminate sexism in the schools.

The provision for the establishment of a council on Women's Educational Programs remained in the proposal. The establishment of this advisory council was considered to be one of the most important aspects of the bill since such a council would be able to oversee all the programs operated by the Office of Education and consequently give women a direct voice into the OE decision-making process.

A Sponsor Is Found and Strategy Set

After completing the drafting of their proposal, the WEAL group needed to find a congressional sponsor for their bill. A number of factors narrowed the list of possible sponsors considerably. The group decided to limit the options to members of the House of Representatives in the belief that they would be more inclined than Senators to devote time to a proposal that was relatively narrow in impact and appeal. The options were further limited to members of the House Select Subcommittee on Education, because the members of this subcommittee would be the ones to whom the bill would almost certainly be referred once it was introduced.[b] Lastly, due to the nature of the bill, the group decided that the sponsor should be a woman. The obvious choice for a sponsor based on these

---

[b]At the time, there were three subcommittees that handled education legislation for the Committee on Education and Labor. The Special Education Subcommittee handled higher education bills, the General Education Subcommittee handled bills on elementary and secondary education and the Select Education Subcommittee handled bills that did not routinely fall into the jurisdiction of the other two subcommittees. In contrast, the Senate had only one subcommittee that handled education bills.

considerations was Representative Patsy Mink (D., Hawaii). Although Mink was not regarded as a feminist, she had high seniority on the Select Education Subcommittee and was believed to be receptive to being identified with a noncontroversial women's equity proposal.

In March 1972, the WEAL group wrote Mink's administrative assistant and explained who they were, how they had come to draft the bill, and why they believed the bill was necessary. Enclosing a copy of their draft bill, they also impressed upon Mink's assistant that they believed she was the only member of Congress who could guide the bill into law. Mink's assistant brought the letter and bill to Mink's attention, and she was immediately favorable to the idea of sponsoring the proposal.

Mink met with Arlene Horowitz in early April in order to discuss the bill's introduction and to set strategy for building support for the proposal. At this meeting, Mink expressed her belief that she should not push for hearings on the bill until the next session of Congress, which would begin in January 1973. The postponement was based on her desire to hold extensive hearings on educational discrimination against girls and women, mainly in elementary and secondary schools, in order to establish on the record the clear need for the bill, as well as to demonstrate the widespread support from women's groups and education groups that the bill would enjoy. Without such hearings, Mink feared the bill would be considered as frivolous or unnecessary since criticism of schools for being sex biased was new and still largely unaccepted.

Since extensive hearings would not be possible during the time remaining in the 92nd Congress, Mink planned to use the immediate introduction of the bill merely as a way of gaining attention for the idea of the bill and as a method for developing support for the proposal. For the same reason, she decided not to attempt to get cosponsors for the bill when she introduced it, but rather planned to concentrate on getting wide cosponsorship when she reintroduced the bill at the beginning of the 93rd Congress. At this meeting, Mink also expressed her desire that the interim period be used to obtain the reactions of women and educators to the bill so that any problems with the proposal could be corrected before she began pushing the bill in earnest.

Mink's strategy was clearly slow and tentative and was based on the belief that a bill aimed at funding programs to improve women's education would need a long and careful process of developing support in order for it to pass. She did not want to invest her time and energies on a bill that would end up going nowhere, or if passed, would never receive an appropriation. Since WEAL group members agreed with Mink's strategy of not lobbying for the bill until the next Congress WEAL had no problem in accepting Mink's approach.

The Bill Is Introduced and Quickly Dies

On April 18, 1972, Representative Mink introduced the Women's Education Act of 1972 after having made only minor modifications in the bill as it was presented to her by the WEAL group.[1]

The bill, as it was introduced, called for:

The establishment of a Council on Women's Educational Programs in the Office of Education;

Curriculum development and the support of women's education programs at all levels of education;

Preservice and inservice training programs, fellowship programs, seminars, symposiums, and conferences on women's education;

Research and development of nondiscriminatory texts and materials, tests, and vocational and career counseling;

Development of new and expanded physical education and sports activities;

The recruitment, training, organizing, and employing of professionals and others to participate in and coordinate women's educational programs;

Programs to increase the number of women in administrative positions at all levels in institutions of education and to increase the number of male teachers in elementary and preschool education.

The bill was given the number H.R. 14451 and referred to the Education and Labor Committee, where it remained, with no action taken on it during the remainder of the 92nd Congress. After introducing the bill, Mink set out on a publicity campaign to develop interest in the bill. In the following months she sent out hundreds of letters to persons WEAL had informed her were likely to be interested in the bill. Mink encouraged the recipients of the letters to write her with suggestions for changes in the bill or simply to express their reactions to it. However, with the exception of short articles on the content of the bill in newsletters put out for educators and women, and a short piece on it in *Ms.* magazine,[2] the bill received little attention from the media.

The bill did come to the attention of Senator Walter Mondale (D., Minnesota), who was on the Senate Education Subcommittee. Mondale called Mink in late April to ask whether he could sponsor the bill in the Senate. The request came as a surprise to Mink, but it was a request she was delighted to oblige since Mondale was on the Senate subcommittee that would have to approve the bill. Since neither Mink nor Mondale chaired their subcommittees, they could not establish any specific strategy on how to move the bill.[c] All Mondale could agree to at this time was to try to get hearings in the Senate on the bill during the next session of Congress.

[c]The reason for this is that the Senator or Representative who chairs the subcommittee has almost total discretion as to which of the large number of bills referred to the subcommittee actually are taken up by the subcommittee. Generally, only members of the majority party with a high level of seniority have much success in getting the subcommittee on which they are on to consider bills they have sponsored. Minority members of the subcommittee and majority members of the subcommittee with low seniority often cannot on their own get their bills considered by the subcommittee. The same is true of members of Congress who sponsor bills that go to subcommittees they are not on.

At the end of August, the WEAL group received information leaked from the Office of Education that OE had decided to recommend that DHEW oppose most of the provisions in the bill. The knowledge that the administration would probably oppose the bill when it was considered during the next Congress merely acted to spur on the efforts of the people working on the bill to develop broad support for it. As part of this effort, WEAL distributed a fact sheet documenting the existence of sexism in education and explaining the provisions of the bill. The fact sheet hammered hard at the inequities in the present system by stating: "Despite the fact that the American educational system has been coeducational for more than 100 years, female children receive inadequate, irrelevant, and inferior education when it is compared to that received by male children." In making the case for the bill, the fact sheet declared: "An intensive effort is necessary to correct an educational system which systematically neglects or suppresses the full talents of American women."

The letters sent out by Mink, the fact sheet distributed by WEAL, and the articles that appeared on the bill, produced a large amount of correspondence addressed to Mink that was supportive of the bill. In September, Mink asked the WEAL group to review all the letters she had received in order to give her recommendations on what changes should be made in the bill prior to reintroduction in January 1973. The WEAL group spent September through December reviewing the correspondence as well as rethinking for themselves how the bill could be strengthened.

By the middle of December, the WEAL group completed its review of suggested changes in the bill. Some of the outside suggestions were accepted and incorporated in the bill. However, most of the suggestions that had been made to Mink were rejected, either because they were ideas that had already been considered and decided against or because the suggestions were based on a misunderstanding of what the bill was trying to do. The WEAL group also made some changes in the bill on their own and turned their recommendations over to Mink, who reviewed the bill and made some additional minor modifications.

The Bill Is Reintroduced in the House and Hearings Held

Since all pending bills automatically died at the end of the two-year 92nd congressional session, it was necessary for the bill to be reintroduced in the 93rd Congress. On January 3, 1973, the first day of the 93rd Congress, Mink reintroduced the bill. The bill was designated H.R. 208 and was again assigned to the Education and Labor Committee.

The most noticeable of the changes made in the 1973 version of the bill from the version introduced the previous year was the change in its name. The bill had been reentitled "Women's Educational Equity Act" after much deliberation on the subject by the WEAL group. The group had wanted to give the bill a name that would better convey what they considered to be the major problem: the lack of equity for women. Since most of the women working on the bill were members of the Women's Equity Action League, it is not surprising that the new title for the bill was quite similar to their organization's name.

Other changes in the bill from the previous year's version included some changes in the duties, responsibilities, and composition of the advisory council to be established; new provisions allowing funds to be used for disseminating materials; and funds for programs aimed at obtaining adequate distribution of both sexes in educational positions. The 1973 proposal also contained an increased authorization level that would bring the funding to $15 million in 1975, $25 million in 1976, and $40 million in 1977.

The subcommittee to which the bill would be assigned in the new Congress was unclear at first, due to the reorganization of the subcommittee structure by the House Education and Labor Committee. The bill eventually was referred to the newly created Subcommittee on Equal Opportunities, of which Mink was now a member and which was chaired by Representative Augustus Hawkins (D., Cal.). Mink immediately contacted Hawkins who assured her that the bill would receive the attention of the subcommittee if Mink so desired.

At Mink's request, the subcommittee set aside two days for hearings on the bill during July and two days in September 1973, and the subcommittee staff in conjunction with Mink's staff set about identifying individual people and groups to testify at the hearings. It was their aim to bring in as witnesses a wide range of highly knowledgeable persons to present hard data on the extent of the problem, while at the same time to demonstrate the extensive support that existed for the bill.

During the July hearings, witnesses for twelve organizations appeared before the Subcommittee on Equal Opportunities.[3] Support for the bill was provided by all the witnesses, who represented a large segment of the national women's and education groups in the country, including: Women's Equity Action League; Association of American Colleges; American Council on Education; National Womens Political Caucus; Association for Supervision and Curriculum Development; National Education Association; Interstate Association of Commissions on the Status of Women; National Council of Jewish Women; National Organization for Women; American Personnel and Guidance Association; National Vocational Guidance Association; and National Student Lobby. The Federation of Organizations for Professional Women also submitted a statement endorsing the proposal for the record.

Besides indicating their support for the bill, these witnesses presented in their testimony a wealth of data documenting the existence of sex discrimination in almost every aspect of education, as well as indicating the widespread efforts being made throughout the country to begin changing such conditions. Clearly, the most impressive evidence entered into the record was the November 1972 *Report of the Commissioner's Task Force on the Impact of Office of*

Education Programs on Women. The Task Force report proved beyond challenge that sex discrimination was a problem of major proportions.

Several of the witnesses, aware of DHEW's opposition to the bill, made particular efforts to justify the need for a separate bill aimed at women's education. For example, Arvonne Fraser, President of WEAL stated:

Some may argue that Title IX is enough, that prohibiting discrimination will end discrimination, WEAL argues that this legislation is an affirmative action plan with money to make it work. It is positive legislation aimed at changing old habits and instituting new ideas, materials, and ways of doing things.[4]

A representative affiliated with the National Education Association contested the view that the programs that would be supported under the bill were duplicative by stating:

The argument may be made that funds are available under other existing programs. Although a few projects have funded programs for women, they represent a miniscule amount of research and demonstration funds awarded by the U.S. Office of Education and the National Institute of Education. Given the current situation of increasing educational costs and a declining Federal support of educational activities, it is naive to assume that systematic programs for increasing women's educational opportunities will be developed without specific designation of funds for these activities.[5]

In total, the testimony given during the two days of hearings in July were impressive for their thoroughness and for the unanimity of support provided by women and education groups for the measure. In order to demonstrate the support the bill had from Representatives, Mink scheduled a day of hearings in September to hear congressional testimony. On August 17 she sent out a "Dear Colleague" letter to the other members of the House inviting them to testify or submit statements on the bill. In addition, she asked whether any of them would like to become a cosponsor of the bill.

Responding immediately to the offer to cosponsor the bill were seventeen Representatives. Eventually a total of twenty-two Representatives were identified as cosponsors of the bill. However, at the September 12 hearing, only one Representative actually was present to testify. As a result, the hearing cannot be considered to have produced an indication of strong or widespread congressional support for the bill. Instead, the hearing demonstrated that while many Representatives had indicated privately to Mink that they supported the bill, their interest was not deep and could not compete with other legislative priorities for their attention or their staffs' time. As such, the hearing probably did little to help the chances of the bill. A final day of hearings was held devoted entirely to sex bias in textbooks. Once again, the witnesses presented extensive documentation to support their charges, this time on the sex-biased portrayals contained in school textbooks.

In spite of excellent testimony presented by a wide range of witnesses, the four days of hearings held before the House Subcommittee on Equal Opportunities did not create much interest or excitement on the part of the subcommittee members for moving ahead with the bill at that time. Because of this, Mink chose to continue her previous strategy of slowly building interest and support for the bill. Rather than pushing it too soon and having it fail, or even worse having it pass but never receive funding, Mink was content to wait and gradually develop the support needed.

The Bill Is Introduced in the Senate and Hearings Held

In September, after the completion of the House hearings, Mondale began preparing to introduce the bill. As Mink had done earlier on the House side, Mondale sent out a "Dear Colleague" letter asking for other senators to join him in sponsoring the bill. When Mondale introduced the bill on October 2, 1973, he had been notified by six senators that they wanted to be listed as cosponsors, which was a respectable number, but certainly not a display of great interest or enthusiasm on the part of other senators.

While Mink had used the passage of ERA as an argument for the bill, Mondale, in his remarks to the Senate in introducing the bill used the passage of Title IX as necessitating passage of the bill. Mondale termed the Women's Educational Equity Act the "logical complement to Title IX." However, he was careful to point out that unlike Title IX, the bill was not coercive, by explaining that "The legislation would not require any teacher or principal, any school district or book publisher, any teacher's union or parent to do anything. It would simply be a source of support to communities, schools, parents, or other groups who believe a discriminatory educational situation exists and want to remedy it."[6]

In October and the beginning of November 1973, hearings were held on the bill (S. 2518) before the Senate Subcommittee on Education of the Committee on Labor and Public Welfare.[7] Some of the same witnesses who had testified before the House testified again and the themes stressed at the Senate hearings were the same as had been raised before the House committee. For example, Bernice Sandler, representing the Association of American Colleges, again emphasized that "Title IX would not provide for a new program to be designed to directly encourage girls to take a course, or to train counselors to advocate the entry of girls into such a course, nor would it train the instructor to deal fairly with the new female students. To merely end discrimination is not enough, new programs are vitally needed to deal with the new issues arising as discrimination ends."[8] Sandler also made the point raised at the House hearings that although DHEW does operate numerous programs that might provide funding for activities concerning women, these programs all have their own priorities that do not include women. Similar testimony was given by Ann Scott of the National Organization for Women. Scott testified: "NOW has serious doubts about HEW's concern whether or not women suffer discrimination in education. Their track record tells the truth about their indifference to women." Scott, like Sandler, concluded that "HEW is not going to move unless Congress requires it to."[9]

WEAL arranged for Billie Jean King to testify on the discrimination she experienced as a girl in sports while she was growing up. Whereas Mondale was the only Senator present at the hearing held in October, five Senators showed up to hear King testify in November. King's testimony resulted in national news stories on the hearing, the most important and extensive news publicity the bill would ever receive.

Also testifying in November was Charles Saunders, Acting Assistant Secretary for Education, who was accompanied by a number of other DHEW officials. Mondale had asked DHEW to testify even though it was obvious that the Department would oppose the bill. Mondale apparently believed that one of the strongest arguments for the bill was DHEW's own inactivity in the area, something that could best be exposed by having Department officials testify at the hearing. After reciting DHEW's efforts in the area, Saunders as expected concluded: "The Administration strongly supports the objective of educational equity for all, but we do not regard the method set forth in the bill for achieving this objective as necessary or desirable. . . . We feel that the stated objectives can be attained through determined efforts under existing authorities and resources available to the Department. . . ."[10]

DHEW's opposition to the bill was clearly part of the "company line" all administration officials were taking at the time in regard to new categorical programs being proposed by Congress. While some effort was made on the part of the women in DHEW to get the Department to make an exception in this case and support the bill, such a position even if agreed to within DHEW would have had to also be approved by the Office of Management and Budget (OMB), which clears all testimony to make certain it is consistent with the administration's position. The chances of getting testimony supportive of the bill cleared by OMB were considered so slight, the women in DHEW were reluctant to push very hard to get the Department to submit a favorable position to OMB for approval.[d] Besides the obvious difficulty of getting a supportive position approved, the women in DHEW were not entirely enthusiastic about the bill. Several members of the OE Task Force on women's education feared that if the bill passed it would be used by OE as an excuse not to devote any other program funds to the problems of discrimination in women's education. For these reasons, no major effort was made internally for DHEW to testify in favor of the bill.

Instead of supporting the bill, DHEW put forward in its testimony a three-part nonlegislative strategy to achieve educational equity for women. This

[d]Later in November OMB did in fact submit a bill report to the subcommittee in which it strongly opposed the bill as "a narrow categorical approach to a broad problem."

strategy included implementing the recommendations made by an OE Task Force on women's education, having the Department's Office of Civil Rights enforce Title IX, and moving forward under existing authorities with projects to equalize educational opportunities for women.

It is ironic that the OE Task Force report concerning women's education was used by both Mondale and DHEW to support their positions. Mondale used the report to prove the existence of a major problem as well as to show OE's lack of action in the area; DHEW used the report to demonstrate its interest in the area and its movement to solve the problem. As part of his efforts to debunk DHEW's promises, Mondale requested that DHEW submit a summary of the actions it had actually taken to implement the recommendations contained in the Task Force report. The summary submitted by DHEW indicated that few mechanisms had been used to implement the recommendations, even where the Department had accepted the recommendations as valid. For the most part, the Office of Education had only made vague future commitments to focus on the problems of women in education. Therefore, the documents submitted by DHEW on the actions taken to implement the Task Force report were anything but supportive of the Department's position on the bill.[e]

After having asked numerous questions regarding DHEW's alternative approaches to solving the problem of sex discrimination in education, Mondale asked Assistant Secretary Saunders whether the administration would be willing to work with him to develop a proposal that DHEW could support. However, Saunders was intransigent and insisted that no compromise was possible since the legislation was unnecessary to accomplish the desired objectives.

By coincidence the next witness appearing before the subcommittee after the administration witnesses was Barbara Kilberg. Although Kilberg was testifying on behalf of the National Women's Political Caucus she also happened to be a member of DHEW's Advisory Committee on the Rights and Responsibilities of Women. She strongly objected to the position taken by DHEW and indicated that the Advisory Council had not been consulted in the development of DHEW's position. If the Advisory Committee had been asked, she indicated it would have strongly urged the Department to support the Equity Act.

The Senate hearings, like the House hearings before them, failed to produce any great interest on the part of other subcommittee members. Since the House hearings had been held such a short time before, the Senate hearings seemed in some ways to be anticlimatic to the groups working for the bill and did not seem to develop any additional interest or support for the Equity Act.

Taken together, the four days of House hearings and two days of Senate hearings served a variety of purposes. Although congressional attendance at both

---

[e]It is somewhat surprising that DHEW did not even attempt to put its record in a better light. The explanation why it did not probably lies with the fact that Assistant Secretary Saunders was personally committed to increased attention to the area of sex bias and, therefore, was not inclined to have the Department slant the record just for the sake of submitting a more favorable assessment of its progress in this area.

sets of hearings was generally quite low, the hearings were well attended by the staff of the subcommittee members and served the extremely important function of educating these staff members about the problem of sex bias in education. The testimony that was presented thoroughly documented the existence of sexism in the schools, particularly at the elementary and secondary school levels. This was especially important since there had been no previous congressional hearings on the problem of sexism in elementary and secondary schools.

The testimony presented also demonstrated the bill's widespread support from women's and education groups. The testimony made it clear that there was a great amount of interest in changing the sex-role stereotypes fostered by the education system and that much greater progress could be made with federal financial support. Furthermore, the testimony also served to prove that DHEW on its own had not, and probably would not, make any major effort in the area. In addition, the hearings impressed upon Congress that the banning of sex discrimination by passage of ERA and Title IX would not automatically improve the situation for women in education and that money would be required to help schools make the desired changes.

It is impossible to measure the impact that the hearings had on Congress. While the support generated by the hearings and the documentation presented were widely viewed as having enhanced the prospects that the bill would receive favorable consideration, if the bill was ever brought before Congress, the hearings were seen as having done little to improve the immediate political prospects that the bill would ever be brought up for a vote due to the bill's comparative insignificance when compared to other educational issues pending before Congress.

In addition to developing possible future support for the Equity Act if it were taken up for a vote, the hearings also served an indirect function of publicizing the existence of sex bias in the schools and legitimizing criticism of the education system due to this bias. The record of the two hearings ran over 1,000 pages, and copies were widely requested by individuals around the country, since they constituted the most comprehensive reference sources available at the time that documented the discriminatory treatment received by women in elementary and secondary education. Although the hearings were not given extensive coverage in national news media, they were given a great amount of attention in the newsletters issued by a number of women's and education groups, thus spurring interest in both the bill and the existence of sex bias in education in general.

The Bill Is Rewritten, Incorporated into an Omnibus Education Bill, and Is Passed

In order to make the purpose and the program objectives of the bill as clear and convincing as possible Mondale's staff decided, even before Mondale introduced the bill, that the bill should be modified and streamlined. The counsel to the Senate Subcommittee on Education also impressed upon Mondale the need to improve the language of the bill. After the Senate hearings, Ellen Hoffman, the staff member of the Senate Committee on Labor and Public Welfare who had been working on the bill, met with Mink and the groups backing the bill to discuss language changes that might strengthen it.

The major problem with the original bill drafted by the WEAL group was that it was considered vague in many areas and contained too many unidentified terms that could be misconstrued, which thus made the bill appear more controversial and threatening than it actually was. Since the suggested changes in the bill mainly involved style, neither Mink nor the women's groups objected to having the bill rewritten. By the end of November, a much shorter version of the bill, containing more precise language, had been drafted. The revised version, for example, had reduced the type of activities to be funded from sixteen specific types of actions to six more general categories of activities.

By the end of November 1973, it had become clear that the Women's Education Equity Act stood its best chance of being immediately considered and adopted by Congress if it were made part of the bill to extend existing elementary and secondary education programs being considered at that time. Since the Senate Subcommittee on Education, rather than House subcommittees on Education, mainly works on omnibus education bills, the chances for successfully tying a new bill into the education amendments was thought to be greater in the Senate than in the House.

Since the Senate subcommittee handles all education legislation, the interests of the members are broader than those of the members of the more specialized House subcommittees. As a result, Senate subcommittee members are more differential to the legislation introduced by the other subcommittee members than is the case in the House. Another result is the more frequent use of legislative log-rolling in order to develop support for a wide variety of legislative proposals by Senate subcommittee members.

Added to the logic of pushing the bill on the Senate side was the fact that the House subcommittees were further along than the Senate subcommittee in their consideration of the education legislation. Therefore, it would have been difficult at this point to get the Women's Educational Equity Act folded into the larger bill being developed by the House. For these reasons, if the bill were to be incorporated into the education amendments, it would have to be done by the Senate Subcommittee on Education.

The bill on women's education was not the only new education proposal pending before the Senate Subcommittee on Education. Various members of the subcommittee had also sponsored bills dealing with such topics as metric education, gifted and talented children, community schools, career education, consumer's education, and art education. These proposals were all being considered at a time when the Nixon Administration was fighting hard to have Congress consolidate existing categorical programs in education into a smaller number of broader grants that gave state and local education agencies greater discretion over how to spend the funds. As the hearings on the Equity Act indicated, the administration was also opposing the passage of new categorical programs. Therefore, the chances of any of the proposals that were only actively supported by a few Senators passing on their own as separate bills was not good. Even if they were included as separate programs in the omnibus education amendments, the probability that all of the new programs would pass was quite low.

How to include their particular bills in the omnibus education package in such a way as to allow them to pass was thus a major dilemma confronting several members of the Senate subcommittee, and not just Mondale. While there was little sympathy in either the House or the Senate for the administration's proposal for major consolidation of programs, there was some acceptance that consolidating some education programs would probably help OE more effectively administer its programs. With these considerations in mind, both the Democratic and Republican staffs to the Education Subcommittee were working on devising a legislative solution to these problems. After much deliberation, the minority Republican staff devised an approach that would solve the problem.

Their proposal called for the seven proposed programs, as well as some existing programs, to be consolidated into a new program for special projects. These new categorical programs would, for an incubator period of three years, be guaranteed 50 percent of the appropriation for the Special Projects Act, with the other 50 percent going for uses selected by the Commissioner of Education. After this three-year period, when the new programs had the opportunity to become established and to prove their worth, they would be moved from the set-aside shelter to the Commissioner's discretionary section and compete for funding with the other established programs consolidated by the Act. Congress could then establish new priority areas to receive funding. This approach assured that the advantages of consolidation would not be eroded by the continuing establishment and perpetuation of new and separate categorical programs.

The new Special Projects Act would authorize a total of $200 million to be spent on the programs in the Act each year for the following three years. In order to prevent the seven new programs from competing with each other for funding during these three years, the proposal had the appropriation for each strictly based on a formula written into the law. The formula that was developed was based on the authorization level requested in the original bills, with the exception of the Equity Act. Unlike the other bills, the Equity Act was given a slightly lower authorization level than its original authorization level warranted, because the subcommittee staff drawing up the proposal thought the original request was too high.

Under the formula suggested for the Special Projects Act, the Women's Educational Equity Act would be guaranteed an appropriation of 15 percent of the total funds appropriated each year. This would amount to $30 million a year if the Special Projects Act was funded for its full $200 million authorization.

The remaining appropriation for the Special Projects Act not spent on the seven new programs was to be spent on whatever areas the Office of Education considered as deserving attention. These discretionary funds could be used by OE to support several education programs that had previously been funded separately, or they could be used for new projects selected by the Commissioner of Education.

Under the requirements of the proposed Special Projects Act, if the Commissioner wanted to continue having funds spent at his discretion, he would have to request funding for the entire Special Projects Act. For example, if he wished to continue funding for such highly popular projects as Sesame Street and the Electric Company television series, he would be required to ask for funding for the entire Act. This would place the Republican administration in a difficult bind: It would either have to eliminate funding for several programs considered of great importance to the administration or request funding for new programs that it opposed for ideological and fiscal reasons.

The Special Projects proposal reflected the belief that it was beneficial to consolidate certain established categorical programs so that OE's program management could change in accord with shifting priorities within the Office of Education. The proposal also represented the belief that it was equally important to make certain that OE responded to newly perceived educational needs and that this could best be accomplished by having Congress mandate several limited categorical programs. The approach devised by the minority staff thus moved in two opposite directions at the same time. It paid token tribute to the administration's position that separate categorical programs should be consolidated, while at the same time it established new categorical programs to focus on specific areas of need.

The proposal developed by the staff was presented to the subcommittee members as merely that: a staff proposal. Mondale had obviously been aware that both the minority and majority staffs of the subcommittee had been trying to come up with some approach to get the seven new proposals through Congress, but neither he nor his staff were involved in the development of the proposal and he knew nothing about its content until it was presented to the subcommittee for consideration. Mondale immediately appreciated the wisdom of the special projects approach, but believed himself obligated to consult with Mink before agreeing that the Equity Act should be among the bills incorporated into the new special projects program. When she was contacted by Mondale, Mink realized that the proposed consolidation was a practical and expedient approach to a very difficult political problem. Still, she was concerned that this method would not give the bill its proper attention. She was also concerned that the approach would not result in Congress focusing its attention on the problem of sex bias in education or result in a clear statement that Congress intended to improve the quality of the education received by women.

As she had done all along, Mink refused to make a decision affecting the bill until she had contacted the groups who were supporting the bill and discussed with them the proposed consolidation approach. These groups shared her concerns, but eventually agreed with her that the consolidation approach was the wisest course of action to follow. If the consolidated approach failed, they knew they could still hold the second year of hearings as originally planned and continue pushing for the bill on its own. Other members of the subcommittee also realized that the proposal was a clever method to get the proposed bills passed with a minimum of opposition, as well as a practical method of guaranteeing that funds would be appropriated to carry out the programs. In the end, the subcommittee members approved the Special Projects Act in nearly the exact form as it had been presented to them by the subcommittee's staff.

By the time that the Women's Education Equity Act was before the full Senate Labor and Public Welfare Committee, it was only a minor section of one part of a complex and major education bill. It would have been highly unusual for such a small and noncontroversial item to even be discussed at the full-committee level, no less rejected by the Committee. It is not surprising under the circumstances that there was little attention paid to the Women's Education Equity Act, or for that matter, the entire Special Projects Act during the full Committee deliberations. Instead, the Committee spent its time discussing such issues as the formula to be used to distribute Title I compensatory education funds, the prohibition of busing for school integration, and the continuation of impact aid to school districts financially affected by the presence of federal workers or property in their school district.

On March 29, 1974, the Senate Labor and Public Welfare Committee reported its omnibus education bill (S. 1539) to the full Senate. Included in the bill reported by the Senate Committee was the Special Projects Act. In its report to the full Senate, the Committee based its support for the Equity Act on the evidence given at the Senate hearings and concluded "that a more vigorous and focused Federal role should be taken in eliminating the widespread sex discrimination in education," and that the program, by providing support for affirmative action programs, would enhance the prospects of full implementation of Title IX.[11] By this time, the House had already considered and passed its own version of the Education Amendments of 1974 (H.R. 69), which did not contain the Women's Education Equity Act or a Special Projects Act. During the five days that the Senate debated the education bill, it focused on the same topics that had earlier taken up much of the Committee's time, such as busing, impact aid, and the Title I formula. The topic of the Special Projects Act was never raised during the course of debate.

An issue that did come up on the floor of the Senate was the ban on sex discrimination in college sports. On May 20, the Senate accepted an amendment, introduced by Senator John Tower (R., Texas), which exempted revenue-producing intercollegiate sports from coverage under the Title IX amendment passed in 1972. Later that day the Senate approved the entire S. 1539 bill; it did so without voting directly on the Equity Act or Special Projects section. Thus, on the same day the Senate passed an amendment seriously weakening the anti-sex discrimination law it had passed in 1972 and voted to start a new program to improve the quality of women's education.

Since the House and Senate versions of the education legislation differed in a number of ways, it was necessary for a House-Senate Conference Committee to meet to resolve the differences. During June and July, the Conference Committee met and attempted to resolve the differences between the House and Senate bills. Both Mink and Mondale were appointed to represent their houses in the Conference Committee. Thus, both the House and Senate sponsors of the Equity Act would be able to participate in the discussions and decisions on the bill. Since the bill was contained in the Senate version, but not the House version, the main responsibility for assuring the bill's acceptance by the conference committee lay with Mink as the House sponsor.

Mink did not think the bill would encounter any serious difficulty in being accepted, but to make certain she encouraged the women's and education groups backing the bill to indicate their support to the conferees. The women's and education groups responded to the call for assistance by making a massive lobbying effort on behalf of the bill. The women, who actually lined the corridors outside the room where the conferees were meeting in order to impress upon the House and Senate members as they came and left that their actions on the Tower Amendment to Title IX were being closely watched, also used the occasion to express their support for the Equity Act. In addition, both Mink and Mondale discussed the bill with their colleagues to assure that it would be supported if a challenge to it were raised.

As it turned out, there was no real controversy over the bill. The conferees, like the committees in both houses before, were overwhelmed with numerous issues considered more important and more controversial. The general feeling expressed by the conferees about the entire Special Projects Act was that it only provided a small amount of funding for a small number of noncontroversial programs and only funded them on their own for a few years. It simply was not worthwhile for the House Conference Committee members to take up valuable time over what was considered to be a minor provision included in the Senate, but not the House, bill. In addition, any attempt to delete one of the seven programs included in the Act would have placed in jeopardy the entire approach. Therefore, unless a Representative was willing to challenge the entire Special Projects approach, the individual programs such as the Equity Act, were really beyond reach. Only a few minor and technical changes, were eventually made before the House Conference Committee members agreed to accept the Senate-passed proposal.[f]

[f]The Conference Committee did greatly modify the Tower Amendment. Instead of excluding revenue-producing sports, the bill as approved by the Conference merely stipulated that DHEW develop reasonable rules relating to participation in intercollegiate sports. For a full discussion of this action, see Chapter 5 of this volume.

Toward the end of July, the Conference Committee completed its work and presented its report to the full House and Senate,[12] both of which quickly passed the bill, again without directly voting on the Equity Act or Special Projects provision. On August 21, 1974, President Gerald Ford in one of his first acts as President signed the Education Amendments of 1974 into law (P.L. 93-380). Nearly three years had passed since Arlene Horowitz originally thought of the idea for the bill and twenty-seven months, since Mink first introduced it, but the Women's Educational Equity Act had finally become law.

Content of the Law

As Section 408 of P.L. 93-380, the Women's Educational Equity Act of 1974 authorized funding for the following types of activities to achieve educational equity for males and females:

Development, evaluation, and dissemination of curricula, textbooks, and other educational materials;

Preservice and inservice training for educational personnel, including guidance and counseling;

Research, development, and educational activities designed to advance educational equity;

Guidance and counseling activities, including the development of nondiscriminatory tests;

Educational activities to increase opportunities for adult women, including continuing educational activities for underemployed and unemployed women;

Expansion and improvement of programs for women in vocational education, career education, physical education, and educational administration.

The law also established an Advisory Council on Women's Educational Programs in the Office of Education to be composed of seventeen members appointed by the President with the consent of the Senate. Also automatically serving on the Council were the Chairman of the Civil Rights Commission, the Director of the Women's Bureau in the Department of Labor, and the Director of DHEW's Women's Action Program. The Council was assigned the responsibility for advising the Commissioner of Education on policy related to the administration of the programs funded under the Act, making recommendations on the allocation of funds, and developing criteria for establishing program priorities. The Council was also given the responsibility of advising the Assistant Secretary for Education on how to improve educational equity for women.[g]

First Steps Are Taken to Implement the Law

In order to implement the Equity Act, the President had to appoint members of the Advisory Council, and the Office of Education had to develop rules governing the expenditure of funds under the Act. In addition, Congress had to appropriate actual funds for the entire Special Projects Act.

Immediately after the Women's Educational Equity Act passed, Mink wrote to the women and educators who had previously expressed interest in the bill to warn them that a concerted effort and a continuing barage of letters to Congress was needed if the Equity Act was to receive an adequate funding level. Actually, the nature of the Special Projects Act practically guaranteed that the Equity Act would receive funding and that affecting the level of funding for the program on an individual basis would be impossible.

On February 3, 1975, President Ford submitted his budget for the following fiscal year to Congress. Out of the $200,000 million authorized to be spent on the Special Projects Act, the President requested only $39 million. This level of funding, which was based on DHEW's request for the program, was derived from the level of funding DHEW wanted for the Commissioner's discretionary authority, rather than out of any concern for how much money was necessary to launch the seven new programs that were mandated in the Act.

Under the formula established in the law, if Congress appropriated $39 million, the Equity Act's share was to be $6.3 million. The fact that this was such a low level of funding for a program aimed at improving the quality of education for 52 percent of the population was raised at both the House and Senate Appropriations Committee hearings held on the administration's budget request.[13] When Commissioner of Education Bell was asked at these hearings how he hoped to achieve equity for women with a "lousy 6.3 million," Bell did not even attempt to justify the figure. Rather, he replied simply that the amount was required by the formula.[h] Bell did not point out that the administration could have used the discretionary funds in the Special Projects Act to increase

[g]The Education Amendments of 1976 passed in October 1976 added to the stated duties of the Council the authority to make reports to the President and Congress and to disseminate information concerning the activities of the Council.

[h]In July 1976 DHEW would submit to Congress an amendment to the Special Projects Act that would have altered this formula. DHEW's proposal would have required only 25 percent of the funds to be spent on the seven Special Project programs, rather than the 50 percent mandated in the law. However, DHEW's proposal was never introduced in either the House or the Senate.

the level of funding for the Equity Act, but had chosen not to do so.[i] Joan Duval, Director of the Women's Educational Equity Office in the Office of Education, did attempt to defend the level of funding by stating that the impact of the money would be stretched since the emphasis of the projects to be funded would be the development of products and modules that could be disseminated widely.

One member of the House Appropriations Committee, rather than thinking the amount was too small, thought it was too much. Representative Robert Michel (R., Ill.) stated that "One of the problems with passing omnibus type of legislation like the Education Amendments of 1974 is that numerous minor items such as this women's educational equity program end up being slipped into the bill without much notice or chance to do much about it at the time, but end up costing the taxpayers millions of dollars."[14] In spite of expressions of concern that the amount of funding might be too low or too high, Congress eventually approved the appropriation level requested by DHEW.

The Advisory Council established by the Act had been the provision that DHEW had objected to most in its Senate testimony, as unnecessary and duplicative of the existing Secretarial Advisory Committee on the Rights and Responsibilities of Women. Although President Ford signed the bill into law in August, by October 1974 he had still taken no action to actually name the seventeen appointed members to the Council. At Mink's instigation, all sixteen women members of Congress signed a letter to the President in October urging him to give his immediate consideration to this matter. In spite of this urging, it was not until the very end of February 1975 that the President finally sent his nominations for the Council to Congress for approval.

It is widely agreed that many of the individuals who were nominated by the President to be on the Council were not particularly interested, experienced, or knowledgeable in the area of women's education. In addition, the proposed composition of the Council was seen as neglecting several major areas of education, particularly the elementary and secondary school levels. It is extremely odd that a Council that was to provide advice on the implementation of law focusing on the elementary and secondary school levels should be heavily dominated by representatives from higher education. Although the composition of the Council concerned many women's groups, they decided that the formation of the Council had been delayed too long already and, therefore, they should not attempt to get Congress to block the nominations or get the President to withdraw them. Instead, they decided to concentrate on getting qualified individuals nominated to replace those members whose appointments ran only one year. While the congressional sponsors of the law were also unhappy with the proposed membership for the Council, they followed the lead

---

[i]The administration would use some of its discretionary funds for career education in addition to the funds mandated for career education programs under the Special Projects formula.

of the women's groups and did not attempt to impede Senate confirmation of the nominees considered to be unqualified.

Due to their late appointment and the inexperience with DHEW's operation of many of the Council's members, combined with the undistinguished credentials of many of its members, the Council got off to a poor start. The late appointment and lack of familiarity with the program resulted in the Council having almost no input into how the first year's money for the program would be spent. By the time the first meeting of the Council was held, OE had already drafted and released its proposed funding pattern.[15] All the Council could do was review the proposed rules governing funding, review the sixty or so public comments that had been sent to DHEW on the rules, and attempt to influence the changes being considered by OE before the final program rules were established. Since the Council had not as yet hired its staff, it would have a difficult time drawing up its comments, no less having an impact on what the final funding rules actually stated.

The Office of Education decided to administer the program utilizing a capacity-building strategy. This approach emphasized funding projects operated mainly by state and local education agencies. This strategy was based on the assumption that meaningful change in the way the education system treats women could best be achieved by having the projects run by the state and local education agencies themselves. Once a program or product had been developed and proven to be effective in one school district or education agency, a major effort would be made to disseminate the end product for adoption elsewhere.

The large variety of programs allowed under the law that the developers of the legislation had purposely placed there, was to cause OE great problems when it had to design an implementation plan for the law. Because of the scope of the programs that could be funded under the broad language contained in the law, the Office of Education was compelled to develop priority areas for funding, rather than attempt to spend equal amounts of money on all the program categories eligible for funding. Based on internal discussions as well as discussions with women's and education groups, five broad areas were finally selected to be the focus of the projects funded during the first year of the program.[16] The priorities selected were: developing training modules, for preservice and inservice training of teachers and other educators, that create an awareness of sex-role stereotyping; supporting programs that prepare women to assume leadership roles in education; supporting programs designed to broaden the career options of women; developing instruments to assist in obtaining compliance with Title IX; and developing a communications network to disseminate information on women's education.

Both the capacity-building approach pursued by OE and the areas selected for funding have been criticized by some women's and education groups as well as by some members of the advisory council. In particular, the fact that most of the money would not be going to women's groups and would not be used to support on-going services was a great disappointment to a large number of local women's groups that had hoped to obtain Equity Act funds to support their activities. The wisdom of these decisions will not be measurable for a number of years, due to the lengthy process involved in developing, testing, and validating the effectiveness of the products produced by the projects.

In the meantime, the portion of the Act that will probably have the most immediate impact will be the Advisory Council. The Council is able to operate with a large amount of autonomy due to the fact that its members are appointed by the President and serve fixed terms. In addition, the Council has a staff responsible to the Council and not to DHEW. The Council has, therefore, an excellent opportunity to make extensive use of its legal authority to monitor the operation of federal education programs as they relate to women. At the very least, the Council will serve as a force that can harass DHEW officials for not devoting sufficient resources and attention to the problems confronted by women in education. At the most, the Council will be able to function as an instrument helping to bring about meaningful reforms in the ways the Office of Education operates on issues relating to the unique problems facing women. To a large extent it appears that the eventual effectiveness of the Council will be determined by its ability to work with the OE policymakers in an advisory, rather than a policy-making, capacity. If the members end up confronting rather than cooperating with OE officials, as was often the case during its first year of operation, the Council will probably end up being little more than an irritant to OE officials.

Despite heavy lobbying by women's groups, the Women's Educational Equity Act continues to be funded at an extremely low level.[j] However, it is still possible that the Act will eventually produce significant and meaningful changes in the education system. Besides the direct impact of the projects funded under the Act and the activities of the Advisory Council, the existence of a federal law on women's education will also have the indirect effect of stimulating additional interest and activity in this area by state and local education agencies and groups. But clearly, it is much too early to assess how significant the passage of the law will be for improving the treatment of girls and women in the educational system.

---

[j]The fiscal year 1977 appropriation for the Equity Act was $7.3 million, $1 million more than had been appropriated in fiscal year 1976. DHEW had requested $400,000 less for the second year's appropriation than had been spent the program's first year. However, this request was ignored by both the House and Senate. The House originally voted to continue funding the program in 1977 at the $6.3 million level, while the Senate originally voted a $3 million increase for the program, thereby bringing it to $9.3 million. Eventually, a House-Senate Conference Committee agreed to a compromise figure of a $1 million increase in the appropriation level for 1977. By increasing the appropriation for the Equity Act, Congress was in effect altering without formal amendment the formula contained in the authorizing statute for distributing funds to the Special Project programs.

Concluding Observations

The way in which the bill was presented to Congress illustrates a number of points about the treatment of women's issues by Congress. The Women's Educational Equity Act could have been presented as a proposal that directly and openly confronted the issue of sex bias in education. Such an approach could have forced Congress to make a decision on whether the problems facing women in education were of sufficient national importance to warrant the passage and funding of a law. This approach would have been similar to the Emergency School Aid Act, which provides over $200 million a year in financial assistance to school districts in the process of eliminating minority group isolation through desegregation. The passage of Title IX in 1972 provided a perfect parallel of Congress to pass the Equity Act to financially assist schools eliminating sexist practices, just as Congress had done earlier in regard to race discrimination in education. Neither Representative Mink nor Senator Mondale used this approach. If this approach had been used and had been successful, the passage of the Women's Educational Equity Act would have provided a major statement on the part of Congress that it recognized the severity of the sexist bias in the schools and, more importantly, was willing to commit substantial federal funds to eliminate it.

For this approach to have been successful, it would have been necessary to make a much greater effort to develop support for the bill. The congressional sponsors would have had to spend much more time working on the proposal and invested more of their personal prestige in the effort. The bill's sponsors also would have had to organize a major campaign to sensitize and educate the members of Congress on the issue of sex bias in the schools. In addition, they would have had to mobilize significantly greater political pressure on the part of the women's and education groups supporting the proposal.

Both Mink's and Mondale's moderate postures on women issues made this more militant approach for presenting a bill unacceptable for them. Also, as political pragmatists, getting a somewhat limited bill adopted immediately would be of more concern to them than the possibility of getting a bill with broader implications and larger funding passed at some time in the future. In addition, neither Mink nor Mondale would be inclined to spend so much time on a bill of this nature, given their numerous other legislative interests and commitments. Even if one of them had been willing to spend the time and make the effort to get this particular bill passed, the approach would have needed the support of both in order to be successful.

If both Mink and Mondale had been willing to make the effort, the chances of this approach being successful still would not be good. Lengthy hearings over a number of years, as originally planned by Mink, could possibly have performed the necessary educative function. However, it appears unlikely that the amount of political pressure necessary to get a bill presented in this fashion through Congress ever could have been developed. The women's groups supporting the bill were at the time just learning how to influence Congress. They also lacked the unity necessary to give them substantial political clout. The education groups supporting the bill clearly did have the membership and financial resources necessary to have substantial influence in Congress on an issue of this type if they chose to use it. However, it is unlikely that a topic such as this, which did not directly affect the well-being of their membership, ever would have been made a high enough organizational priority to bring about the mobilization of support needed to get the bill through Congress. For these reasons, it appears that this aggressive approach would have been extremely time-consuming and most likely would have resulted in failure in the end in any case. If the most important end product of the legislative process on this issue was the immediate passage of the Women's Educational Equity Act, and the approval of some funds to operate its programs, then this approach certainly made little sense. However, the reasons this approach was not taken, and could not be, if the bill were to pass, is in itself illustrative of the extreme difficulty of having legislation favorable to women passed by Congress.

The alternative method for presenting and pushing the bill, and the route used by both Mink and Mondale, involved portraying the bill as a small, noncontroversial, and limited program. This approach did not require more than a few members of Congress to ever become knowledgeable about or active on the proposal in order to have it enacted. Moreover, since the bill was not presented in a threatening fashion, other members of Congress had no incentive to spend time on the matter. This approach basically allowed Congress to pass the bill under the guise of merely giving women's interest groups their fair share of education funds, in much the same manner as the demands of other special interest education groups were handled. The bill also provided an inoffensive piece of legislation that members of Congress could vote for and later use for political purposes as an indication of their support for "reasonable" legislation for women. It would thus be less difficult politically for these members of Congress to vote to weaken Title IX or work against other proposals benefiting women in other legislative areas.

If the bill was indeed seen by some members of Congress as just giving women's interest groups their due, then women were certainly bought off extremely cheaply. Similarly, if the bill was seen as a sop to women thus freeing Senators and Representatives to oppose more important initiatives benefiting women, then the value of getting the bill through in this fashion must be viewed in a much harsher light.

The approach eventually taken—including the bill in a larger consolidated Special Projects bill—further diluted the symbolic value attached to having the bill passed. As it was presented, there was no real consideration of the problem of sex bias in education or, more importantly, any discussion of the merits of using federal funds to help eliminate the problem. Instead, the personal political influence of Mondale and Mink were the major factors involved.

If the bill had continued to be presented on its own as originally introduced by Mink, then at least it could have forced Congress to make a decision on the merits of the issue no matter how nonthreateningly the issues were couched. It is unclear, however, whether the bill could have been passed and funded on its own even using this nonthreatening approach. Possibly after several years of hearings, after building support among interest groups, and after Mink and Mondale made use of their influence, the bill might have been passed.

As the bill was presented, the problems facing girls and women in education were never firmly planted in the congressional conscience. The subsequent efforts to weaken Title IX, and the difficulty experienced by the women groups in turning back these efforts, illustrates this clearly. Thus, the presentation of the bill in this fashion managed to obtain for women a $6-million program, but certainly no lasting educative or political impression was made on Congress that could carry over and assist women in their efforts to obtain legislation in other areas.

The events surrounding the enactment of the Women's Educational Equity Act did, however, have one important byproduct. The activities engaged in during the course of congressional consideration of the bill provided one of the first opportunities for women to meet and work politically with other women who were concerned about sexism in education. The actions taken by the groups involved on this issue constitute the first attempt at a lobbying coalition of women and educational groups. The involvement of women and educators concerned with the elementary and secondary levels is particularly significant since almost all prior legislative activity had focused on sex bias in higher education. As such, the involvement brought about by the Women's Educational Equity Act clearly helped develop a basis for increased communication between these groups on women's education issues. The formation of a broad and almost formal coalition, which would later show its strength on Title IX, can directly be attributed to the impetus provided by the actions surrounding this bill. Therefore, the formation of an effective women's lobby on education issues constitutes a legacy that may be, in the long run, a more important end product on this issue than the actual passage of the Women's Educational Equity Act itself.

Notes

Except where otherwise footnoted, the information presented in this chapter was obtained from interviews with persons listed below and documents provided by them. Also indicated is the capacity in which these people were interviewed.

Of necessity, the material presented in the chapter relies on the authors' interpretation of the information obtained from these sources.

Interview with Susan Grayson, staff member of the House Subcommittee on Equal Opportunities, November 1975.

Interview with Bernice Sandler, former Vice President of WEAL and current chairperson of the Advisory Council on Women's Educational Programs, November 1975.

Interview with Joan Duval, Director of the Women's Educational Equity Program, U.S. Office of Education, October 1975.

Interview with Ellen Hoffman, staff member of the Senate Committee on Labor and Public Welfare, October 1975.

Interview with Holly Knox, former Director of the U.S. Office of Education Women's Education Task Force and current member of the Council on Women's Educational Programs, October 1975.

Interview with Carol Burris, Director of Women's Lobby, Inc., October 1975.

Interview with Arlene Horowitz, former staff member of House Committee on Education and Labor and Director of WEAL's Project on Equality in Education, October 1975.

Interview with Susan Kakesako, Legislative Assistant in the Office of Representative Patsy Mink, October 1975.

Interview with Roy Millenson, former staff member of the Senate Subcommittee on Education, October 1975.

1. 118 *Congressional Record* 13159-61, April 18, 1972.

2. Virginia Kerr and Ellen Sudow, "Call to Action: A Legislative Agenda for the 93rd Congress," *Ms.* (January 1973), pp. 81-85.

3. For the full text of the testimonies discussed in this section, see U.S. House of Representatives, *Hearings Before the House Subcommittee on Equal Opportunities, Committee on Education and Labor on the Women's Educational Equity Act*, 93rd Congress, 1st Session, Washington, D.C., 1973.

4. Ibid., p. 17.

5. Ibid., pp. 231-32.

6. 119 *Congressional Record* 32483-92, October 2, 1973.

7. For the full text of the testimonies discussed in this section, see U.S. Senate, *Hearings Before the Senate Subcommittee on Education, Committee on Labor and Public Welfare on Women's Educational Equity Act of 1973*, 93rd Congress, 1st Session, Washington, D.C., 1973.

8. Ibid., p. 49.

9. Ibid., p. 72.

10. Ibid., pp. 100-01.

11. *Senate Report*, No. 93-763, 93rd Congress, 2nd Session, Washington, D.C., 1974.

12. *House of Representatives Report*, No. 93-121, 93rd Congress, 2nd Session, Washington, D.C., 1974.

13. For the full text of the testimonies discussed in this section, see U.S. House of Representatives, *Hearings Before the House Subcommittee on Departments of Labor and Health, Education, and Welfare, Committee on Appropriations, on Education and Related Agencies Appropriations, Fiscal Year, 1976* 94th Congress, 1st Session, Washington, D.C., 1975; and U.S. Senate, *Hearings Before the Senate Committee on Appropriations on Educational Division and Related Agencies Appropriations, Fiscal Year 1976*, 94th Congress, 1st Session, Washington, D.C., 1975.

14. Ibid., *Hearings Before the House Subcommittee on Appropriations*, p. 908.

15. *Federal Register*, August 11, 1975.

16. *Federal Register*, February 12, 1976.

5

Sex Discrimination and the Administrative Rule-Making Process: The Development of the Title IX Regulation

The history of the development, enactment, and initial implementation of Title IX, the federal law banning sex discrimination in education, spans a seven-year time period (1970-1976). During these years, the issue of sex bias in the schools, which had previously been of interest and concern mainly to women's rights advocates, was transformed into a major public policy issue, largely as a result of the controversy surrounding this law. At one point or another over the past seven years, every branch of the federal government has been involved in the policy-making process on Title IX. Because of the number of years covered, different actors involved, and variety of actions that have taken place, the history of Title IX is necessarily complex. The meandering path of policy making on Title IX illustrates quite clearly that what in 1970 appeared to be a relatively simple aim to achieve (equal treatment of the sexes in education) has turned out to be an extremely difficult and elusive goal to actually attain. The following case history documents why this has been so.

A Legislative Proposal Is Developed and Introduced in the House

During the 1950s and 1960s Congress passed a number of laws that provided financial aid to both institutions of higher education and their students. Many of these laws were scheduled to expire in 1971. In 1970, various Representatives and Senators began introducing bills to extend and expand these higher education programs. At this time, Representative Edith Green (D., Ore.), who was head of the House Special Subcommittee on Education, which had jurisdiction over higher education, introduced a higher education bill that would have significantly increased the federal support given to colleges.

At the time when Green was developing her bill a number of events would bring the issue of sex discrimination in education to the public's attention. For example, the Women's Equity Action League filed a class action administrative complaint against hundreds of colleges and universities that had contracts with the federal government and charged them with violating the executive order prohibiting sex discrimination. In addition, a presidential task force on women's rights and responsibilities issued its report that documented the existence of sex bias in American society and recommended numerous legislative changes to ban sex discrimination in education as well as other areas. It appears that these events prompted Green to include in her higher education bill provisions to prohibit sex discrimination. In fact, three of the provisions Green included in her bill had been specifically recommended by the presidential task force.

The bill Green proposed would have removed the existing exemption of education from the antidiscrimination ban in Title VII of the Civil Rights Act of 1964; amended the 1957 Civil Rights Act to authorize the U.S. Civil Rights Commission to study discrimination against women; and would have removed the existing exemption from coverage of executive, administrative, and professional employees under the equal pay for equal work provision of the Fair Labor Standards Act. In addition to these changes recommended by the task force, Green included in her bill a much more sweeping ban on sex discrimination. Green was using the higher education bill as a vehicle for amending the Civil Rights Act of 1964 to expand its coverage to prohibit discrimination on the basis of sex in all federally financed programs. The total impact of Green's sex discrimination proposal, if it had been enacted, would have been far-reaching: Sex discrimination in all federal programs would have been prohibited, and protection against sex discrimination in employment would have been greatly expanded.

During June and July of 1970, Green held hearings on her sex discrimination proposal.[1] These were the first congressional hearings ever devoted to the issue of sex discrimination in education. During the seven days of hearings, overwhelming evidence was presented by women's groups to document discrimination against female graduate students and faculty members by colleges and universities and to show that without federal legislation protecting them, women would in all likelihood continue to be discriminated against. However, most major education organizations did not testify at the hearings because they apparently did not consider the issue to be of sufficient importance to warrant their attention. In addition, the hearings were not well attended by the subcommittee members.

Green's omnibus education bill, of which the sex discrimination provisions were a part, never went further than the hearing stage. Under no pressure to act to extend programs that did not expire until the following year and lacking a consensus among themselves as to the appropriate role for the federal government in assisting higher education, the members of the Special Subcommittee on Education were unwilling to act on Green's proposal.

More Congressional Proposals Are Introduced

At the start of the next session of Congress in January 1971, several Senators and Representatives again introduced higher education proposals. In the Senate, a Democratic-endorsed bill was introduced by Senator Clairbourne Pell (D., Rhode Island), who chaired the Senate Subcommittee on Education. The Pell bill (S. 659) did not contain any sex discrimination provision. However, a Nixon Administration supported-proposal, which was introduced in the Senate, did contain a section that would have prohibited sex discrimination in federally assisted education programs and activities except where sex was a bona fide ground for differential treatment.

In the House, Representative John Brademas (D. Indiana), a member of the Special Subcommittee on Education, who had disagreed with numerous aspects of Green's 1970 higher education proposal, prepared and introduced his own proposal in 1971. The bill introduced by Brademas included a sex discrimination provision that, like Green's, was based on the recommendations made by the task force on women's rights and responsibilities. Brademas' proposal contained only two amendments, both of which had been proposed by Green in 1970. The administration's proposal that had been introduced in the Senate was also introduced in identical form in the House by Representative Albert Quie (R., Minn.).

Green's proposal was the third major higher education proposal introduced in the House. The sex discrimination provisions in Green's 1971 higher education bill were significantly different from the provisions contained in her 1970 proposal. Instead of amending the Civil Rights Act of 1964 to prohibit sex discrimination in all programs receiving federal financial assistance, Green's 1971 proposal would ban sex discrimination only in federally assisted education programs. In addition, the 1971 proposal to amend the 1964 Civil Rights Act contained several exemptions that had not been included in the previous year's bill. The 1971 bill totally exempted from coverage substantially single-sex institutions and institutions that were controlled by a religious organization where the discrimination provision conflicted with the religious tenets of the organization.[a] In addition, the 1971 version allowed education institutions that were in the process of changing from single-sex enrollment to coeducational five years before they would be covered. The 1971 proposal also contained a provision to add education employees to those covered by Title VII of the Civil Rights Act. Besides these provisions, Green's 1971 bill contained in identical form the three other provisions that had been in her 1970 bill.

By the middle of July 1971, the Senate Subcommittee on Education and the full Labor and Public Welfare Committee had completed work on an omnibus education proposal and ordered the bill reported to the Senate for consideration. The bill agreed to by the Senate Committee, like the bill introduced by Pell, did not contain a provision concerning sex discrimination.

The absence of a sex discrimination provision in the bill appears to have resulted more from oversight than design. The administration's bill, which did contain an anti-sex discrimination provision, was never seriously considered, and none of the Education Subcommittee or full Committee members appeared to

[a]It appears that the provision to exempt substantially single-sex schools was included mainly due to Green's desire for the seven sister women's colleges to be exempted from coverage.

have any strong personal interest in the sex discrimination issue. Thus, the problems resulting from sex discrimination in education were never really considered. Instead, the Committee members devoted their energies to working out solutions to the large number of other issues that had to be considered and resolved in the omnibus education bill.

In the beginning of August the full Senate began considering the bill approved by the Labor and Public Welfare Committee. At this time both Senator Birch Bayh (D., Ind.) and Senator George McGovern (D., S.D.) introduced amendments to ban sex discrimination in higher education programs. The Bayh amendment contained a provision prohibiting sex discrimination by public undergraduate colleges and universities and both public and private graduate schools receiving federal funds. Under the Bayh proposal, colleges changing from single sex to coeducational were allowed seven years before they would be required to admit students in a nondiscriminatory way. With this exception, all other colleges would be required to admit students based on their qualifications without regard to sex. The second major provision in the Bayh proposal was an amendment to Title IV of the 1964 Civil Rights Act. This amendment would allow the Attorney General to file suit on behalf of persons who had been denied admission to a college because of their sex. This proposal had been among those recommended by the task force on women's rights and responsibilities. Although not one of Bayh's stated intentions, this amendment would subsequently provide the basis for the Office of Education's using the funds appropriated under Title IV for training and technical assistance activities to overcome sex as well as race discrimination. Lastly, the Bayh proposal required the Commissioner of Education to conduct a nationwide survey to determine the extent of sex discrimination in education, a proposal also recommended by the Task Force. The amendment submitted by McGovern was similar in many ways to Bayh's proposal, but was more limited in scope.

The introduction of the amendments by Bayh and McGovern brought the total number of different anti-sex discrimination proposals introduced in the House and Senate to five. The approaches taken in these proposals to combat sex discrimination in education varied greatly. In all, proposals were reintroduced to amend the Civil Rights Act of 1957; Titles IV, VI, and VII of the Civil Rights Act of 1964; several provisions in the Fair Labor Standards Act; and the Higher Education Act of 1965. The proposals also varied greatly in the coverage and exemptions. The varied content and scope of these proposals indicates that basic agreement was lacking as to what constituted the best approach to take in order to eliminate sex discrimination in education. There also was obvious disagreement about how far the federal government should go in prohibiting policies and practices that treated the sexes differently.

The Senate Considers the Bayh Amendment

In the midst of the Senate debate in August 1971 on the education amendments, Bayh asked to have his amendment considered.[2] At this time McGovern indicated he would not ask for his amendment to be taken up, but would instead support Bayh's proposal. As such, McGovern's amendment was never considered by the Senate.

The impact that Bayh's amendment would have on specific types of schools—such as military schools, divinity schools, and public women's colleges— was the chief concern expressed during the brief floor debate on the amendment. Due to the absence of any legislative hearings or previous debate on the amendment, a number of Senators expressed confusion about the impact the amendment would have on admissions policies. Repeatedly, Bayh explained that the proposal did not require schools to admit equal numbers of males and females and that admission quotas of any kind were prohibited under the provisions of the amendment. Bayh emphasized that all the proposal would require was admissions to be based totally on the merit of the applicant without sex of the applicant being considered.

Before taking up the entire education bill, the Senate, in order to speed up consideration of the bill, had unanimously agreed that all amendments introduced on the floor had to be germane to the provisions already in the bill. After hearing Bayh's responses to questions about the amendment's impact on military and single sex schools and college admissions policies in general, Senator Strom Thurmond (R., S.C.) stated that he opposed the amendment both because of its specific provisions and because of his concern about concentrating so much power in Washington over the states' operation of higher education. Thurmond then raised a point of order questioning whether Bayh's amendment was germane to the education amendments being considered. Senator Walter Cannon (D., Nev.), who was chairing the Senate at the time, ruled that Bayh's amendment was not related to the bill under consideration and therefore could not be considered.

Bayh, who was obviously totally unprepared for this parliamentary move, appealed the ruling of the chair to the full Senate. Bayh argued that the entire higher education bill dealt with the issue of equal access to education, and therefore his proposal was related to the contents of the bill. In contrast, Thurmond argued that Bayh's amendment was very broad and would change the entire complexion of many institutions and that hearings should be held and the implications of the amendment fully understood before it was considered. In the vote that followed, the ruling of the chair was upheld by a 50-32 margin. The Senate went on the same day to unanimously approve the higher education bill and sent it to the House for consideration.

With the defeat on procedural grounds of the Bayh amendment, the opportunity to insert a sex discrimination provision in the Senate's version of the higher education bill seemed to have ended. As such, the failure of the Bayh amendment could have been a critical blow to the hopes of women wishing to ban sex discrimination in education. The reasons for the failure of the Bayh amendment are numerous. The failure of the Senate subcommittee members to hold hearings on or consider the issue of sex discrimination had placed the entire burden of developing the proposal and raising the issue on Bayh. To some observers the proposal that Bayh developed was not carefully drafted from either a political or a legal perspective. In addition, it appears that Bayh did not do a very good job of presenting the arguments for the amendment or clearing the way for its consideration. Considering the support his proposal had, Bayh probably should have been able to get the amendment considered and adopted. Instead, poor drafting and sloppy political handling resulted in the amendment never actually being voted on by the Senate.

House Considers Green's Proposal

At the time the Senate was considering and passing the higher education amendments in August 1971, Green's education subcommittee was still working on developing a House version of the bill. On the sex discrimination issue the House subcommittee had to decide between the approaches suggested by Green, Brademas, and the administration. Green, after introducing her bill in 1971, apparently had some doubts about the wisdom of amending Title VI of the 1964 Civil Rights Act to include a ban on sex discrimination. Such a proposal might set a precedent for offering amendments to Title VI and therefore open it up to weakening amendments proposed by members of Congress opposed to its impact on racial policies. Instead, Green decided it would be better to ban sex discrimination through a separate provision inserted in the education bill that was modeled after the language of Title VI. During the subcommittee deliberations, Green was successful in getting the subcommittee to adopt this approach.

The most politically difficult issue for the subcommittee to resolve was whether to cover college admissions policies, and if so, how to cover them. Green's proposal covered all admissions policies with the exception of institutions that were substantially single sex. Various other possibilities, suggested by subcommittee members, included: covering admissions policies only for higher education; covering admissions policies only for public institutions; covering admissions policies only for graduate schools; or not covering admissions policies at all. Representative Quie, in particular, was adamant that admissions policies should be exempt and argued that schools should be allowed to use their admissions policies to create whatever education climate they wanted. Quie, with the support of the Republicans on the subcommittee and some of the Democrats, was eventually successful in getting the subcommittee to vote to exempt all undergraduate colleges' admissions policies from coverage.

Green had apparently expected no difficulty in getting her Democratic colleagues on the subcommittee to defer to her wishes on the issue and as a result had not asked women's groups to lobby in favor of her proposal. However, after the subcommittee's negative action on the admissions issue, Green did request that women's groups work to develop support for her proposal among the members of the full Education and Labor Committee. The women's groups proceeded to engage in an intensive lobbying effort and heavily utilized sympathetic female congressional staff members to place personal pressure on the Representatives for whom they worked.

Near the end of September 1971, the Education and Labor Committee began its deliberations on the education bill developed by the subcommittee. During the consideration of the sex discrimination provisions in the bill, Green moved to have the undergraduate admissions policies' exemption from coverage deleted from the bill. In its place, Green proposed including her original provision covering admissions policies except where the students were substantially all of the same sex.[b] By a vote that closely followed party lines, the committee deleted the former exemption and adopted Green's substitute provision. The lobbying activities of the women's groups and the pressure from female congressional staff members had clearly been effective in developing support for the proposal and had even managed to convince several Democrats who had opposed Green at the subcommittee level to vote for the proposal. Following this action, the committee went on to adopt the entire sex discrimination section as it had been introduced by Green.

At the end of September the committee voted to send the education bill to the House for consideration. However, nine Republican members of the committee attached a statement of dissent from the committee's proposed bill in regard to the sex discrimination section. The Republicans stated that they had deep concern about the provisions affecting enrollment admissions policies because they represented further federal restrictions and controls over institutions of higher education.[3]

The day after the committee voted to send the education bill to the House, Representative John Erlenborn (R., Ill.) introduced an amendment similar to the provisions previously approved by the subcommittee to exempt undergraduate college admissions policies from coverage. In the beginning of November, the House began debate on the sex discrimination section (Title X) of the education bill.[4] Representative Celler, who chaired the Judiciary Committee, immediately objected to the House's considering the provision in the bill that would allow the U.S. Civil Rights Commission to study sex discrimination. Celler argued that this provision should be considered by his committee before being voted on by the House. As a result, this provision was deleted from Title X.

Following this action, Erlenborn asked to have his amendment to exempt undergraduate admissions policies considered. This amendment would have the effect of exempting the admissions policies of 95 percent of the higher education institutions in the country from coverage. Despite forceful opposing arguments by Green as well as by Representatives Patsy Mink (D., Hawaii) and Bella Abzug (D., N.Y.), the Erlenborn amendment was adopted by the House by a 194-189 margin.

---

[b]The Committee defined "substantially" as meaning an enrollment of 90 percent or more of one sex.

When the entire education bill was voted on later the same day, opponents of the Erlenborn amendment had another chance to defeat it but again fell short, this time by a 186-181 margin. The House then went on to pass the education bill and inserted the language of the House bill under the Senate's bill number (S. 659) and sent the bill back to the Senate. Since one of the titles in the bill preceding the sex discrimination section had been defeated by the House, Title X in the bill was renumbered Title IX.

Senate Reconsiders Sex Discrimination Provision

The higher education bill passed by the House differed greatly from the version that had earlier been passed by the Senate. In late November 1971, the Senate decided to have its Committee on Labor and Public Welfare consider the provisions in the House bill and conclude what, if any, changes should be made in the Senate bill before sending it to a House-Senate conference. Bayh was thus given an unusual second chance to get his sex discrimination amendment considered by the Senate. At this time, Bayh indicated to the Senate that as a result of consultations with other Senators, he had modified his proposal in order to meet the objections raised during the earlier debate on the proposal.[5] For example, Bayh now proposed that exemptions be made of the admissions policies of religious schools as well as those undergraduate colleges where 90 percent of the students were the same sex. Bayh's amendment was still broader in coverage than the House-passed version since it would have covered the admissions policies of most undergraduate colleges. Bayh, who was not a member of the committee considering the bill, tried to obtain a commitment from Pell that as committee head he would support Bayh's amendment. However, Pell did not commit himself.

The Senate Education and Labor Committee worked on reconsidering the higher education bill over the next several months and eventually sent it back to the full Senate near the end of February 1972. Although the bill was modified in a number of areas from the earlier Senate-passed bill, it still did not contain a sex discrimination provision.

At the end of February 1972, during Senate debate on the revised education bill, Bayh asked to have considered his anti-sex discrimination amendment. Bayh's proposal by this time had been changed from the one he had introduced in November. His proposal now contained the key provisions from his earlier amendment as well as many of the features from the version passed by the House.

Bayh's amendment allowed for no exemptions in terms of protection against sex discrimination in services available to students within an institution or in employment within an institution. However, in the area of admissions, Bayh proposed to exempt entirely academic elementary and secondary schools, military schools, and religious schools, as well as private undergraduate institutions. Bayh explained that including the exemption for elementary and secondary schools was necessary because "no one even knows how many single-sex schools exist on the elementary and secondary levels or what special qualities of the schools might argue for a continued single sex status."[6] He explained that the exemption granted to private undergraduate colleges was based on those colleges' claim that a change to "sex-neutral admissions policy would be disruptive both in terms of the academic program and in terms of psychological and financial alumni support."[7] Since he did not have sufficient information to counter these claims, Bayh proposed to exclude private undergraduate colleges until Congress had the opportunity to study the issue in greater depth. According to Bayh, the rationale for exempting military schools was purely political, since this exemption would "greatly increase the chance of getting the measure passed."[8]

Unlike the hostile Senate reaction to Bayh's amendment when originally proposed, the response this time was supportive. Clearly, Bayh had done an excellent job of building political support, and as a result Pell, the sponsor of the education bill, was obliged to support it. The Senate, by a voice vote, then easily passed the Bayh amendment. The next day, March 1, the Senate passed the entire education bill and sent it to conference with the House to resolve the differences with the House-passed bill.

Provision Is Approved in Conference and
Passed by Both Houses

The House-Senate Conference Committee took until the end of May to resolve all the differences between the bills. In all, the conferees had to agree on solutions to over 250 differences in the bills, eleven of which involved the prohibition against sex discrimination. The accompanying table presents the major differences between the House and Senate bills on sex discrimination as well as the Conference Committee resolution of these differences.

The bill that emerged from the Conference Committee in May 1972 generally contained the language from the stronger Senate bill. There was little opposition to the proposal in general since the exemption of private undergraduate admissions policies had assuaged the concerns of private colleges. Most of the higher education community spent their time trying to influence the outcome on other sections of the bill that they considered to be more important than the issue of sex discrimination. Without any organized opposition, and with Green pressing hard for adoption, the Conference Committee quickly adopted Title IX without giving much consideration to its eventual impact.

On May 22, 1972, the Senate and on June 8, 1972, the House passed the Conference Committee bill with little debate. President Nixon signed the

Major Differences Between House and Senate Bills and Conference Committee Resolution of the Issues

Provisions in House Bill	Provisions in Senate Bill	Provisions in Bill Approved by Conference Committee
1. Exempts from coverage admissions policies of all undergraduate colleges.	Exempts from coverage admissions policies of private undergraduate colleges, elementary and secondary schools (except vocational schools), military schools, as well as traditionally single-sex public undergraduate colleges.	Contains provision from Senate bill.
2. Exempts entirely those institutions changing from single sex to coeducation.	Exempts those institutions changing from single sex to coeducation only in terms of admissions policies.	Contains provision from Senate bill.
Exempts from coverage those institutions making transition to coed for seven years.	Exempts from coverage all institutions for one year, those making transition to coeducation for an additional six years.	Contains both House and Senate provisions.
3. None.	Exempts military schools from coverage entirely.	Contains provision from Senate bill.
4. Stipulates that nothing shall be interpreted as requiring preferential treatment towards the members of one sex.	None.	Contains provision from House bill.
5. Allows federal funds to be withdrawn as a result of discriminatory employment practices only in those cases where the funds were provided explicitly fro the purpose of providing employment.	None.	Does not contain provision.
6. Repeals exemption of educational institutions in Title VII of the 1964 Civil Rights Act.	Repeals exemption of educational institutions in Title VII of the 1964 Civil Rights Act; exempts institutions with regard to employment of individuals of a particular religion to perform work connected with carrying out religious activities.	Contains provision in House bill.

Provisions in House Bill	Provisions in Senate Bill	Provisions in Bill Approved by Conference Committee
7. None.	Amends Title IV of the 1964 Civil Rights Act to cover sex, thus authorizing the Attorney General to bring suit in sex discrimination cases and allowing Title IV funds to be used to help end sex discrimination.	Contains provision in Senate bill.
8. None.	Authorizes Civil Rights Commission to investigate sex discrimination.	Does not contain provision.
9. None.	Requires study of sex discrimination in education.	Does not contain provision.
10. Specifies that institutions may maintain separate living facilities on the basis of sex.	None.	Contains provision in House bill.

Education Amendments of 1972 on June 23 (P.L. 92-318), and on July 1, 1972, the law went into effect.

DHEW Begins to Develop the Proposed Regulation

At the time that the President signed the Education Amendments of 1972, the Department of Health, Education, and Welfare had not begun any preliminary planning on how to implement Title IX. This was not unusual, since DHEW at this time had no management system for initiating the planning necessary to implement laws. The staff of DHEW's Office for Civil Rights (OCR), where the responsibility for developing the implementing regulation would be assigned, had been generally aware of the existence of Title IX, but had not taken too much interest in it prior to passage. OCR was used to civil rights-oriented legislation getting introduced and considered by Congress but not finally enacted. Understaffed and overloaded with work from enforcing other civil rights laws, OCR had made a general practice of expending little effort on bills that had not yet been passed.

As a result of these factors, OCR did not begin to work on Title IX until a month after it was signed into law. In July 1972, OCR, which had only limited experience enforcing anti-sex discrimination requirements in regard to faculty and no experience in regard to students, attempted to take some preliminary steps to sort out what it had to do to implement Title IX. To a large extent OCR, although organizationally a part of the Office of the Secretary in DHEW, was used to operating with almost total autonomy within the Department. As a result, although some marginal efforts were made to involve and consult DHEW staff outside OCR, for the most part the early decisions on how to begin the implementation process were all made by OCR staff in collaboration with the lawyers in DHEW's General Counsel's office who worked on civil rights issues.

At the initial meeting held to discuss Title IX in July, OCR officials decided that the preparation of a draft regulation should be used as a vehicle for raising important policy issues. It was also decided that a letter should be sent by the Department to all education institutions affected by Title IX informing them of the new law.

In August 1972, the memo to be sent to institutions affected by Title IX was sent out to colleges and university presidents. The memo contained no specific guidance on what the regulation would eventually require in terms of policy changes that would have to be made. Instead, the memo merely contained a recitation of the content of the statute. Being inexperienced in the area of sex discrimination, and lacking any guidance from the Secretary of DHEW or President Nixon on what the implementing regulation should require, OCR decided it should not go beyond the language of the law in its official notification to institutions. The same type of general statute-based letter that was sent to the higher education officials was sent by OCR to chief state school officers and local superintendents of schools in November 1972. Thus, next to no guidance would be provided by OCR to schools and colleges about the impact of Title IX prior to the publication of the proposed regulation in 1974. As a result, few schools or colleges initiated policy changes during this time period.

OCR, which not only realized that its staff was generally uninformed on the topic of sex discrimination, but was aware of the controversy likely to be produced by the regulation, arranged a series of meetings beginning in August 1972 with major women's, education, athletic, and student groups as well as school and college officials to discuss the development of the Title IX regulation. In all, more than fifty organizations sent representatives to participate in the discussions on the regulation. From OCR's perspective, these sessions proved to be a great disappointment. Most of the groups attending were far more interested in finding out from OCR what would be required of them than in offering suggestions on how to write the regulation or what should be covered.

By November 1972, a first draft of the regulation to implement Title IX had been prepared by the General Counsel's office and was circulated to various offices within DHEW for review and comment. The draft was only twenty-eight pages long and was basically a cut and paste version of the existing regulation covering race discrimination under Title VI of the 1964 Civil Rights Act, after which Title IX was modeled. Because the Title VI regulation was extremely general in working and vague in terms of requirements, this initial draft of the Title IX regulation also was characterized by these features.

The response to this initial draft was extremely critical from the other DHEW offices that reviewed it, all of which wanted the regulation to be much more specific. Since the President was required by the law to approve the regulation, OCR also sought the views of the White House staff on whether the regulation should be vague like Title VI or contain more detail in content.[c] The White House response indicated that it wanted the regulation to be written with specific indications of policy, but made it clear that it was retaining the option of going with a general regulation when they saw what OCR formulated in terms of specific policies. This decision by the White House staff appears to have been based on the knowledge that the Title VI regulation was so vague that it provided inadequate notice to school districts as to what was required and would thus lead to numerous enforcement disputes. Obviously, the White House also realized it would have more control over the policy requirements on sex discrimination if the requirements were written specifically into the regulation than if they were decided by DHEW unilaterally.

Following the criticism of the draft regulation within the Department and based on the guidance provided by the White House, OCR and General Counsel staffs went back to work on the regulation. Because of the absence of an extensive legislative history, exactly what Congress had intended when it passed the law was unclear in many areas. In addition, there was only a limited amount of case law on sex discrimination in education from which legal precedents could be drawn for determining the policies to be incorporated in the regulation, which thus made it difficult for OCR to decide on the content of a detailed regulation. For guidance in the development of the regulation, the OCR and General Counsel staffs decided to rely heavily on legal and administrative precedents established in enforcing Title VI to determine the scope and coverage of the Title IX regulation.

Once the decision was made to write a detailed regulation based on Title VI precedents, the regulation-writing process should have been able to proceed at a rapid pace. However, the drafting of the Title IX regulation was not made a high priority within DHEW: Only two lawyers in the General Counsel's office were assigned to work on Title IX and this assignment was given to them in addition to their other on-going responsibilities.

Coverage of Private Undergraduate Professional Colleges Becomes An Issue

While the regulation-drafting process proceeded, it was also necessary for DHEW to take another step to implement Title IX. The law required single-sex schools covered by the law to submit transition plans to the Commissioner of Education and to detail the way they planned to eliminate sex discrimination in their

[c]A similar requirement that the President approve the implementing regulation was contained in Title VI. Such a requirement is unusual and seems to reflect a desire on the part of Congress to provide a political check on DHEW's actions in these sensitive areas.

admissions policies. The transition plan had to be submitted, by law, one year from the date Title IX went into effect in order for the school admissions policy to remain exempt from coverage during the six-year transition period allowed them by statute. Although the law specifically granted the authority for approval of the plans to the Commissioner of Education, OCR pre-empted the decision-making responsibility on this matter. In March 1973, OCR asked Secretary Weinberger to decide whether private undergraduate institutions of higher education offering professional programs should be prohibited from discriminating in admissions policies.

Up until this time, all of the activities and decisions on implementation had been made without involving DHEW Secretary Caspar Weinberger. This pattern of handling as many issues as possible below the secretarial level continued throughout the regulation development process and was consistent with Secretary Weinberger's overall management approach. Only those issues on which there was staff disagreement or those that were thought to be highly controversial or important were presented to Weinberger for his decision.

DHEW's dilemma in making the decision on coverage of private undergraduate professional colleges arose from the fact that the legislative history of Title IX could be interpreted as supporting the view that Congress intended for all private undergraduate institutions to be excluded from coverage, but a reading of the exact language of the statute indicated that all professional schools should be covered. Normally, when the language of a statute is as clear as it was in this case, the statute's wording is all that would be considered when deciding how to implement the law. However, in this instance, the Office for Civil Rights, the General Counsel's office, and the offices of the Assistant Secretary for Education and Assistant Secretary for Planning and Evaluation disagreed among themselves as to how the Department should proceed. Weinberger sided with OCR and the General Counsel's office and decided that DHEW should follow the intent of Congress and exclude all private undergraduate colleges from coverage on their admissions policies. As a result, private undergraduate colleges offering programs in professional areas such as engineering, education, and social work would be allowed to continue to discriminate in admissions policies. Not until May 1973 did DHEW finally send out the memos to selected schools and colleges explaining the required content of transition plans for eliminating sex discrimination in admissions policies. At this point, the schools had only one month to submit the required plan if they wanted to take advantage of the exemption from coverage they were entitled to under the law. Due to DHEW's slowness in acting, the transition plan issue was of little consequence since only a handful of colleges actually submitted plans and none were ever officially approved by the Commisssioner of Education. The exclusion of private undergraduate professional schools greatly limited the number of schools affected. The one-month time period allowed to those few schools covered served to discourage those that were affected from taking the process seriously.

The progress made on developing the regulation in general during early 1973 was substantially slowed down by the absence of a permanent director for OCR. The OCR staff and the GC staff working on Title IX were unsure who had the real decision-making authority. As a result, issues of policy and procedure were often left unraised and unresolved for long periods of time. Since Title IX had been passed with, and subsequently received, little congressional or public attention, little pressure was placed on DHEW to act more quickly in developing the regulation.

Secretary Weinberger Becomes Involved in Resolving Controversial Issues

In June 1973, OCR raised in a memorandum another series of issues for the Secretary to decide. One of the issues dealt with the requirements regarding competitive varsity sports and physical education classes. Again, OCR pointed out that the legislative history provided few clues to congressional intent and that the case law was also limited. A second issue brought up was what exceptions, if any, from coverage should be allowed to protect personal privacy. It was pointed out that the statute provided no exceptions, but that the legislative history could be interpreted as supporting exceptions in such cases as restrooms, showers, and possibly physical education and sex hygiene classes. Another issue regarded the extent to which the involvement of schools with and the use of school facilities by private groups that discriminated on the basis of sex (such as fraternities, civic groups, and boys' and girls' groups) should be covered by the regulation. The Secretary was informed that the legislative history was silent on this issue but that DHEW had consistently construed Title VI of the Civil Rights Act as forbidding any institutional support of a private group that limited its membership on the basis of race. However, it was also pointed out that there existed a different legal basis for banning race and sex discrimination. A number of alternative policies was presented to the Secretary by OCR on each of these three issues.

Confronted with differing opinions from various DHEW offices on the issues involved, Weinberger, in a typical maneuver, did not select any of the alternatives offered to him on two of the issues. Instead, he informed OCR in July in a somewhat contradictory response that he favored the development of a regulation policy that gave women an equal opportunity to compete in sports, but that did not give women any more than that. He explained that schools should be required to let women try out for noncontact sport teams but that if they failed to make the team the school should not have to set up a separate women's team for them. At the same time, the Secretary specified that he wanted to allow all male football teams to continue to exist.

On the issue of covering private organizations, Weinberger in July also rejected all of the alternatives provided him in the June action memorandum and asked OCR to develop a much tighter definition of what was meant by school support for outside organizations. He partially defined support, by indicating that the regulation should state that allowing the Boy Scouts to use a school auditorium did not constitute support. He also indicated that he did not believe it was a major obstacle to administer Title IX and Title VI differently on this matter. Weinberger made it clear that it was his belief that federal education funds should be used to provide financial assistance to education, not to reform every organization that used a school auditorium or other school facility.

On the personal privacy issue, Weinberger did select one of the alternatives offered to him in the June memorandum. The Secretary indicated that he saw no basis for treating physical education classes or personal hygiene and sex education classes differently from other courses. Weinberger also stated that the proposed regulation should state that if the public wanted an exemption for physical education or sex education classes, so that they could be offered separately to both sexes, the public should call on Congress to pass such an exemption.

The attitudes expressed by Weinberger in these initial decisions were consistent with the views he manifested throughout the entire regulation development process. Weinberger seemed to believe DHEW should write the regulation without concern for the political reaction of Congress or interest groups. He seemed to want the contents of the regulation to be legally justifiable and sound public policy and appeared less concerned whether the regulation would be politically popular. Still as a political appointee, Weinberger had to be sensitive to political pressure and at times he did make decisions based on political considerations. However, for the most part within the range of options available to him given the language of the statute and political realities, Weinberger was free to make policy decisions that were consistent with his own personal and political value system. Although there were some exceptions, the result was the development of a generally conservative regulation.

DHEW Offices Battle Each Other Over The Content of the Proposed Regulation

Based on the Secretary's comments and decisions, OCR proceeded to revise and develop further the content of the regulation. In August 1973, OCR submitted the proposed regulation to the Secretary's office for the Secretary to approve. The regulation submitted had been developed almost entirely by OCR in collaboration with the General Counsel's office. Other offices in DHEW, including the offices of the Assistant Secretary for Planning and Evaluation and Assistant Secretary for Education, clearly resented that they had not been involved more closely in the drafting process and objected to numerous provisions in the regulation that was presented to the Secretary for his approval. In an apparent effort to avoid having the Secretary become embroiled in a dispute between the various offices, the Secretary's executive office decided not to submit the OCR draft regulation to the Secretary. Instead, they sent it back to OCR for additional work before submitting it to the Secretary for approval.

After the proposed regulation had been returned to OCR for additional work with instructions to involve other DHEW offices, OCR staff realized that they would not be able to totally decide the regulation's content if they wished to receive the Secretary's approval. Weinberger simply would not accept the regulation unless there was substantial staff agreement on its content. As a result, extended discussions and negotiations regarding the content of the regulation were begun between OCR and other DHEW offices, with these meetings often resulting in shouting matches between the tense participants.

A major reason for the dispute between the various DHEW offices was the fact that the participants had quite different views on the significance of the positions to be expressed in the proposed regulation. OCR and the General Counsel's office, which had drafted the regulation and were quite happy with it, primarily wanted to get the proposed regulation published: Internal departmental differences could be resolved later. However, the other offices involved were greatly concerned with what they considered to be the generally weak content of the proposed regulation. In addition, these offices believed that any later changes in the regulation would, for political reasons, be changes to weaken the regulation even more. Therefore, their priority was to get approved a strongly worded proposed regulation, even if publication would be delayed. After several months of staff negotiations, as well as discussions between the various office heads, consensus on most of the issues was finally reached through compromise.

An exception to this decision-making process was the issue of coverage of sex bias in textbooks. This issue was decided personally by the Secretary following a letter to Weinberger in April 1974 from the president of a major university in his home state of California. The university president objected to the requirement that schools and colleges review textbooks for sex bias, which was contained in a draft of regulations that OCR had distributed informally for comment to outside groups. In response Weinberger, in an unusual move, personally drafted a letter in April 1974 without consulting with his staff, in which he indicated that he had not been aware of the language in the draft regulation (although his staff was certain he had been) and that he certainly opposed its covering textbooks. He assured his friend that no such requirement would ever be approved by him.

Following the Secretary's decision not to cover textbooks, the General Counsel's office developed the legal rationale to justify this decision. The General Counsel's office, which had previously worked hard to develop a provision that avoided constitutional problems, now sent out a memo to OCR and other offices and indicated that upon closer review, the wording in the draft regulation requiring curriculum review for sex bias raised grave constitutional questions because of the right of free speech guaranteed by the First Amendment. The General Counsel further indicated the draft language would be changed to exclude entirely any requirement in this area.

In the beginning of May, the General Counsel's office circulated within the Department a revised, but soon-to-be final, draft of the proposed regulation. At the end of May 1974, while HEW was preparing for publication of the proposed Title IX regulation Senator John Tower (R., Texas) was moving to have an amendment to the Title IX law adopted that would exempt revenue-producing intercollegiate sports from coverage. This amendment, which was based largely on the recommendations of the National Collegiate Athletic Association (NCAA), would let teams in revenue-producing sports keep the funds they produced to run their program with only surplus funds used for other men's and women's sports teams. The amendment would help assure that Title IX did not cause revenue-producing sports, such as football and basketball, to lose their financial base by having the money they raised filtered off to other sports programs. The NCAA had previously organized a massive letter-writing campaign to convince the President and DHEW to exempt football and basketball from coverage under the Title IX regulation. The introduction of the amendment to achieve legislatively this objective appears to have been resorted to only after the NCAA became convinced that it could not get the regulation written the way it wanted.

In presenting the proposal, Tower contended that his amendment would actually help women's teams since they sometimes relied on the money raised from men's football and basketball teams to finance their teams. However, the opposing argument was that since not all of these teams siphoned money to women, the amendment could also result in extravagantly financed teams in these two sports, with little or no money left over to help support women's teams. It also would be nearly impossible to devise a system to uniformly determine when a team was actually revenue producing.

On May 20, Tower introduced his proposal as an amendment to the Education Amendments of 1974, which were under consideration by the Senate. He was successful in getting the amendment adopted without debate by a voice vote with only a few Senators present. Since the House version of the education amendments did not contain a similar provision, this issue would become one of the more than two hundred points of difference that existed between the House and Senate versions of the education bill, which a House-Senate Conference Committee would have to resolve later that summer.

Finally, on June 18, 1974, DHEW released the proposed regulation to implement Title IX, two years after it became law. The proposed regulation covered school and college policies in three basic areas: admissions, treatment of students, and employment. Covered in the admissions section of the regulation were schools of vocational education, professional education, graduate higher education, and public institutions of undergraduate higher education. The proposed regulation basically required that comparable efforts be made to recruit students of each sex and that individuals not be treated differently because of sex in the admissions process. Although some schools were exempt with regard to admissions, all schools were required to treat students once they were admitted in a nondiscriminatory manner. This aspect of the regulation generally covered: access to and participation in courses and extracurricular activities (including athletics); eligibility for and receipt of benefits, services, and financial aid; the use of school facilities; and rules governing student housing. All full- and part-time employees were covered by the proposed regulation that prohibited employment discrimination in recruiting; hiring; promotion; tenure; termination; pay; job assignments; granting of leaves; fringe benefits; selection and support for training, sabbaticals, and leaves of absence; employer-sponsored activities; and all other terms and conditions of employment.

At the press conference Weinberger held to announce the release of the proposed regulation, he indicated that the Department would allow public comments on the regulation to be submitted for four months, rather than the more standard thirty days, in order to provide ample time for public consideration of the issues involved and to allow time for school officials who were on vacation for the summer to prepare comments when schools reopened in the fall. As was expected, a large portion of the questions asked of the Secretary at the press conference concerned the issue of college sports, which Weinberger jokingly indicated must be "the most important subject in the United States today."[9]

However, another topic—coeducational sex education—gave the Secretary the most obvious difficulty at the press conference. Although Weinberger had been specifically briefed prior to the press conference on the regulation's coverage of sex education, Weinberger was visibly upset by the questions asked regarding the implications of the regulation. Possibly as a result of the personal discomfort Weinberger felt during the press briefing, he indicated soon after that sex education instruction should be allowed to be offered separately for each sex and had the proposed regulation amended accordingly.[10] In doing this, Weinberger in effect reversed his previous position of July 1973 and now maintained that the rights of privacy would be invaded by requiring coeducational sex education classes.

Congress Considers Limiting the Effect of the Law

In July 1974, the House-Senate Conference Committee considering the Education Amendments of 1974 agreed to replace the Senate-passed Tower Amendment on revenue-producing sports with substitute language suggested by

Senator Jacob Javits (R., N.Y.). The Javits substitute stipulated that the Title IX regulation should include reasonable provisions concerning participation in intercollegiate athletic activities. The rejection of the Tower amendment by the Conference Committee was a major victory for women's groups that had made an all-out lobbying effort to influence the conferees.

The Conference Committee also agreed to a little-noticed House-passed provision that gave Congress forty-five days after the publication by DHEW of final education regulations to disapprove the regulation by a concurrent resolution if it determined that the regulation was inconsistent with the law passed by Congress. This newly expressed right of Congress to, in effect, veto executive department education regulations became a major factor once the Title IX regulation was made final by DHEW.

In October 1974, the House of Representatives voted to adopt an amendment to a supplemental appropriations bill for the Departments of Labor and DHEW. The amendment introduced by Representative Marjorie Holt (R., Md.) was adopted by a 200-169 vote and would have among other things prevented DHEW from gathering any information about sex and race discrimination in educational institutions, thereby effectively keeping DHEW from enforcing Title IX and Title VI. Holt had quietly and carefully lined up political support for her amendment and was assisted in this effort by Representative Edith Green. Green, who had been the House sponsor of Title IX, was upset by the interpretation DHEW had given to the law in its proposed regulation and as a result was working to negate the impact of the law she had previously worked so hard to get passed. Holt and Green, in lining up support for the amendment, showed themselves to be politically adept at exploiting the widespread feeling of resentment felt by many Representatives about the way DHEW had been enforcing civil rights laws in general.

Because the Holt amendment had received little previous attention, it was difficult for the women's groups to muster much of a lobbying effort against it once it was introduced in the House. After the passage of the Holt amendment by the House, women's and civil rights groups combined their efforts to influence the Senate Appropriation Committee, which was by that time considering the House-passed supplemental appropriations bill. These efforts paid off when the Senate Committee a week later voted to delete the Holt amendment from the appropriations bill it passed. Although the women's groups and other civil rights groups were successful in defeating Holt's proposal at this time, the amendment was not dead, and the groups had to engage in even greater efforts to try to defeat it when it was considered again later in 1974.

The Public Deluges DHEW with Comments

In October, the four-month public comment period on the proposed regulation came to an end with an unprecedented total of nearly 10,000 written comments submitted to DHEW. The overwhelming majority of comments submitted to DHEW were written by people who had little expertise in the area. Most of the comments expressed either general support or opposition to the idea that the federal government should require equal treatment of the sexes in education, often without expressing knowledge that a law passed by Congress required DHEW to develop the regulation in the first place. The individual comments were often part of letter-writing campaigns organized by state or local conservative political organizations or by women's organizations.

The comments that DHEW was most concerned with were those submitted by national organizations representing education, women, athletic, teacher, student, and civil rights constituencies. In addition, the comments sent in by state and local public school officials and college and university administrators were reviewed quite closely. These comments were generally written with great care in the belief that the federal policymakers were seriously interested in the writers' views and could be swayed by legal opinions, research evidence, or just plain logic. The DHEW officials, in turn, took these comments very seriously, and a number of the comments that presented ideas and views not previously considered by the DHEW staff, or new legal or educational arguments, were directly responsible for policy changes made in the regulation by DHEW. Representatives from OCR as well as other offices in the Office of the Secretary considered these comments at length, generally by meeting three or four times a week for several hours at a time to review and discuss the comments. The heads of these offices also met informally to discuss the progress of the comment review and redrafting process. As the offices that were involved considered different issues, the blocs supporting particular positions kept shifting, and as a result, there were no permanent alliances pushing for stronger or weaker positions. Instead, conspiratorial-type meetings were held among the staff members who were in agreement on a particular policy position to plot strategy and develop arguments to get their position adopted by the other offices involved and by the Secretary.

The views expressed in the public comments provided no consensus among the groups affected by the regulation as to what policies DHEW should require. The organizations representing women's, teachers', students', and civil rights organizations expressed views advocating much stronger national policies against sex discrimination than did the organizations representing elementary, secondary, and higher education administrators and officials.[11] Because of the absence of any kind of consensus, DHEW policymakers felt free to decide the issues as they thought best from legal and policy perspectives.

Decisions Made on Content of Final Regulation

During November and December 1974 and January 1975, DHEW officials wrestled with the options available to them. OCR, in collaboration with other offices, prepared several decision memos for the Secretary on the most controversial and important issues, including: requiring fringe benefits for part-time workers; requiring coeducational physical education classes; requiring equal pension benefits at the same cost for both sexes; covering sex bias in educational materials and curricula; prohibiting universities from administering scholarships that were awarded on the basis of sex; covering the admissions policies of private undergraduate professional schools; as well as numerous issues relating to athletics and physical education. Some of these issues were raised for the Secretary for the first time, but others had gone previously to the Secretary for decision. These issues were raised again either because there was such strong staff disagreement with an earlier decision of the Secretary or because there was sufficiently strong public sentiment opposing a position contained in the proposed regulation to warrant the Secretary's considering the issue once more. Issues other than these were resolved at the staff or Assistant Secretary level through informal discussions and negotiations.

On most major issues decided personally by the Secretary, the position selected was the most conservative and least desirable from the perspective of women's groups. As had been predicted earlier by some DHEW staff members, the final regulation was to be considerably weaker than the proposed regulation in a number of key areas, and more forceful in only a few areas. Staff-level decisions made on other issues also generally rejected the recommendations of women's groups for stronger and more far-reaching requirements than had been included in the proposed regulation.

Congressional Efforts to Limit Impact of the Law Continue

While DHEW officials were determining the policies to be included in the final regulation, congressional efforts to change the original Title IX law continued. At the end of November, the Holt amendment again became an issue when a House-Senate Conference Committee in a surprise move voted to accept the House-passed amendment as part of a DHEW supplemental appropriations bill. Confronted with House members who insisted on retaining the Holt amendment, the Senate members on the Conference Committee agreed to a compromise to break the deadlock. The committee voted on November 26 to delete the section of Holt's proposal that would have prohibited DHEW from cutting off federal aid to schools that refused to maintain records on the sex (and race) backgrounds of teachers and students. As approved by the Conference Committee, the amendment still would have prohibited DHEW from cutting off federal aid to schools that refused to carry out DHEW orders concerning the assignment of teachers or students on the basis of sex (or race).

In a show of support for the Conference Committee's action, in early December the House voted to reaffirm its October decision backing Holt's amendment. Despite lobbying efforts by women's and civil rights groups, the House passed the amendment by an even greater margin than it had in October when these groups had been able to make only a minor effort to influence the vote.

The women's and civil rights groups now had to focus all of their efforts on the Senate in order to keep the Holt proposal from passing. Senate Majority Leader Mansfield (D., Mont.) and Minority Leader Scott (R., Pa.) cosponsored an alternative amendment that provided that no part of the Holt amendment would stop DHEW from withholding federal aid when such a move was necessary for the enforcement of antidiscrimination laws, thereby making the Holt proposal meaningless. With efforts to weaken or nullify the Mansfield-Scott proposal being unsuccessful, Senators supporting the Holt amendment engaged in a filibuster, a procedural technique to achieve what could not be achieved by a direct vote. In mid-December, the Senate voted to stop debate by a margin of only one vote more than the two-thirds vote needed to invoke cloture and halt debate. Subsequently, the Senate went on to pass the Mansfield-Scott amendment by almost the same two-to-one margin.

The rejection of the Holt amendment by the Senate placed the House under great pressure to pass the appropriation bill as it had been approved by the Senate. Only by accepting the Senate version of the bill could the House pass the bill before Christmas recess and thus ensure that the President, who opposed it because the spending level was too high, could not pocket veto the bill while Congress was not in session. Faced with solid Senate opposition to the Holt amendment and anxious to have the opportunity to override the expected presidential veto, the House finally gave in and voted to approve the appropriation bill with the Mansfield-Scott amendment in it.

The pressure on Congress to exempt fraternities and sororities and youth organizations from coverage under Title IX continued to build as a result of constituent pressures. In order to forestall greater efforts to weaken Title IX, Senator Bayh sponsored an amendment to allow university-based social fraternities and sororities to continue as single-sex organizations. In addition, the amendment would allow schools to continue to sponsor and assist single-sex youth service organizations whose members were chiefly under age nineteen. Bayh's sponsorship of this amendment appears to have been based on his belief that this issue was not important enough to endanger support for Title IX in general. Bayh's proposal was carefully drafted so that it did not apply to recreational groups such as the Little League or to single-sex adult organizations, such as the Jaycees. Bayh's proposal was also written so that the employment practices of the single-sex organizations would remain covered by Title IX even if their membership policies were not protected. Bayh's amendment also differentiated between professional and social fraternities and sororities and exempted only the latter from coverage. Bayh's amendment faced little opposition and was adopted by the House and Senate in December 1974. The women's groups did not actively oppose passage because they did not want to attack Bayh publicly since he had been supportive of and had worked hard for numerous women's rights proposals. Also, the issue of social fraternities and sororities was seen by these groups as so sacred to American society that the women doubted that they could keep Congress from exempting them from coverage even if they engaged in an extensive lobbying effort. Since the scope of Bayh's amendment was limited to an acceptable degree, the women's groups remained inactive on the issue and watched the amendment pass.

Women's Groups Pressure DHEW to Enforce Law

While congressional efforts were underway to weaken Title IX, women's groups were waging their own campaign to urge DHEW to begin enforcing the law even though a final regulation had not yet been issued. The efforts by these women's groups, however, were largely unsuccessful as DHEW did not begin systematic enforcement of Title IX until the major policy issues were resolved and a final regulation published. Frustrated with DHEW's lack of enforcement of Title IX as well as Executive Order 11246, and aware of the precedent in the race area where DHEW had been ordered by the courts to investigate race discrimination complaints promptly, several women lawyers developed the idea of filing a lawsuit against DHEW, charging the agency with not meeting its legal obligations to enforce Title IX and other civil rights laws that covered women.

At the end of November, the Women's Equity Action League and four other groups joined together to file suit in U.S. district court in Washington, D.C., charging that DHEW, as well as the Department of Labor, had failed to enforce antisex discrimination laws.[d] The suit, which was the first ever brought to require the government to enforce anti-sex discrimination laws, asked the district court to order DHEW and the Labor Department to begin concentrated enforcement programs and to use the authority of the Departments to cut off federal funds if necessary to obtain compliance with the antidiscrimination requirements. The suit specifically charged that DHEW had failed to take even threshold steps to begin enforcing Title IX. Although subsequently important, the lawsuit had no immediate impact on the development or enforcement of the Title IX regulation.

Final Regulation Is Cleared with the White House

On February 28, 1975, Weinberger sent the final draft of the Title IX regulation to President Ford for his approval along with a memorandum explaining the

---

[d]The suit when originally filed was referred to as *Women's Equity Action League* v. *Weinberger*. Secretary Mathews became the defendant in the case when he replaced Weinberger as head of DHEW.

major issues involved. The regulation and the memorandum to the President were supposed to be secret documents, and DHEW took numerous precautions to keep knowledge of the documents from leaking out. In spite of the precautions taken, several individuals in DHEW with access to the documents sent a copy to a women's group leader who in turn distributed copies to other leaders of women's organizations. As a result, word on the content of the regulation began to leak out almost immediately, and within weeks a full summary of the regulation had been widely circulated among women's groups. Shortly thereafter the entire text of the regulation was printed in newsletters prepared for educators.

The women's groups were generally distressed with what they considered the very weak nature of the regulation's requirements. They were particularly bothered by the requirement that individuals complaining about sex discrimination utilize the internal grievance procedure established by a school before DHEW would act on a complaint. This provision had not been included in the proposed regulation, and the women's rights groups had not been aware that DHEW was even considering such a requirement. Had it not been for the leak of the regulation submitted to the President, the women would not have learned about the provision until it was made public in the final regulation signed by the President.

Upon learning of this procedural requirement, the women's groups immediately joined to send a telegram to the President asking to meet with him to discuss the regulation. The telegram went unanswered, but after numerous other efforts to reach the President, the White House finally responded to the women's groups and told them to contact a staff member of the President's Domestic Council instead of the President. The initial efforts to meet with the Domestic Council staff member were also unsuccessful, and the women's groups then began a campaign to obtain such a meeting. Women who were prominent Republicans and who were interested in women's rights were contacted and asked to use their influence to help arrange a meeting. The staffs of several members of Congress were also contacted and asked to use their influence with the White House to have a meeting arranged. Apparently as a result of these efforts, the Domestic Council staff changed their position and agreed to meet with representatives from the women's groups to discuss the regulation. Prior to the meeting, the women's groups submitted a lengthy issue paper outlining the areas in the regulation they considered were in greatest need of change.

Most of the actual meeting time was devoted to the grievance procedure issue, but the provisions regarding athletics and scholarships were also discussed. In addition, a new proposal put forward by the women's groups that schools be required to make a self-evaluation of their policies to determine the existence of sex discrimination was discussed at length. When the meeting ended, the women's group leaders had no idea what, if any, changes would be made in the regulation by the White House.

At the end of April the Domestic Council prepared material to brief the

President on the content of the regulation and on issues that were still unresolved. At first it appeared as though DHEW and the Domestic Council were going to take different positions on several issues, but agreements were eventually worked out on most topics. Of particular importance was DHEW's agreement to go along with the self-evaluation requirement supported by the Domestic Council. DHEW also was convinced by the Domestic Council staff to drop the requirement that internal grievance procedures be utilized prior to filing a complaint, although it was decided that the regulation would still continue to require schools to establish an internal grievance procedure process. The Domestic Council staff and DHEW continued to disagree on one issue: whether foreign scholarships should be covered under Title IX. Eventually this issue was presented to the President to resolve. After listening to a heated discussion of this issue between the Domestic Council and DHEW staffs, the President decided to side with DHEW and allow schools to continue to nominate male students for Rhodes scholarships, and as such the final regulation reflected this policy. In a compromise gesture it was also decided that the final regulation should indicate that schools participating in the Rhodes scholarship program had to provide comparable scholarships for women students.

While the White House and DHEW were finalizing the regulation, another congressional effort was being made to restrict by legislative amendment the scope of the regulation. On April 17, after only a brief floor debate, the House overwhelmingly passed an amendment sponsored by Representative Robert Casey (D., Tex.) to a supplemental appropriations bill prohibiting DHEW from withholding federal funds from schools that did not offer physical education classes on a coeducational basis. The amendment also would have allowed youth service organizations and social and honorary fraternities and sororities to continue restricting their membership to only one sex. Although the coverage of social fraternities and sororities in the Casey proposal duplicated the earlier Bayh amendment, it appears that part of the support that the Casey amendment received was based on the mistaken belief by the Representatives that they needed to vote for the proposal in order to exclude these social groups from coverage under the Title IX regulation being drafted by DHEW. However, the Senate, as it had done earlier with the House-passed Holt amendment, subsequently refused to go along with the Casey amendment, thus making the issue one of numerous issues to be resolved by a House-Senate Conference Committee later that summer.

On May 27, the President signed the final regulation and later forwarded it to Congress for review. The regulation was scheduled to go into effect on July 21, 1975, over three years after the day the law containing Title IX went into effect. The basic requirements and coverage of the final regulation were similar to those contained in the proposed regulation with major policy changes having been made in only a few areas. However, numerous smaller policy changes generally made the requirements in the final regulation weaker than those that had been put forward in the proposed regulation.

New Civil Rights Enforcement Plan Proposed by DHEW

On the same day that the final Title IX regulation was officially released to the public, DHEW published a notice in the *Federal Register* of proposed rule making to consolidate the enforcement of all the Department's statutory civil rights responsibilities, including enforcement of Title IX.[12] The publicly stated aim of this new enforcement approach was to allow DHEW to focus on systemic forms of discrimination rather than to respond to individual complaints received in the mail regardless of the seriousness of the individual issue. DHEW wanted to be able to concentrate its limited civil rights staff capacity on what it considered to be the most important and widespread problems since it believed this would result in the greatest amount of significant change.

Women's and civil rights groups had not known about this proposed consolidated procedural regulation until just before its release by DHEW and were as a result extremely bitter about the secrecy with which it had been developed. The fact that DHEW could develop a major change in its civil rights enforcement procedure in total isolation from all the groups effected by it amazed and angered the civil rights and women's groups. To the women's and civil rights groups DHEW seemed to be retreating from its civil rights responsibilities since individual people no longer would be guaranteed by law, if not in fact, that their complaint would be investigated. The women's and other civil rights groups believed that DHEW was not motivated by a genuine desire to improve civil rights enforcement, but rather by a self-serving desire to get out from under the court order regulating its race discrimination enforcement activities.

Women's Groups Debate their Position on Title IX

Under the provisions of the Education Amendments of 1974, Congress had forty-five days to review education regulations to determine whether they were consistent with the law passed. During this time period, Congress could pass a resolution by a majority vote of both Houses disapproving the regulation and ordering DHEW to redraft it before it went into effect. The Title IX regulation became the first test of this new congressional procedure of reviewing education regulations. However, the emotionalism attached to an issue such as sex discrimination made this a poor topic to test out a procedure when Congress was uncertain of the procedure's operation.

With the final approval by the President of the Title IX regulation, the women's groups had to decide whether to support or oppose a congressional resolution disapproving the regulation. So dissatisfied were the women's groups with the final regulation that serious consideration was given to opposing the regulation as being too weak and flawed to be effective. At a meeting attended by representatives of about two dozen groups concerned about equal rights for women in education, the position the groups involved in this coalition should take was debated. Although a number of organization leaders initially urged that the groups adopt a position opposing the regulation, it was eventually unanimously decided that all the groups in the coalition would endorse it.

This decision was based on the fear that DHEW might delay reissuing the regulation for a long period of time if it were rejected by Congress. In addition, the groups in the coalition were uncertain whether a regulation revised by DHEW after congressional rejection would be stronger or weaker than the initial version. They realized that DHEW would be receiving conflicting signals from Congress' rejection of the resolution, since some members would vote against it because they believed it to be too strong and others would vote against it because it was too weak. The women's groups were also concerned that the regulation would become caught up in a lengthy court test if Congress rejected the regulation, since the administration had previously challenged the constitutionality of the provision in the law that allowed Congress to veto administrative regulations. As a result, it was possible that DHEW would take the position that the regulation was in force even if Congress disapproved it. This position undoubtedly would have led to court action by Congress, with the enforcement of Title IX pending the outcome of the case. The women's groups were also concerned that school and college administrators would interpret a congressional rejection of the regulation as a sign that they could continue to discriminate against women. For all of these reasons, the groups in the women's coalition concluded that it would be wisest to support the regulation as signed by the President. After deciding to support the final regulation, the groups in the women's coalition proceeded to urge Congress to let the regulation go into effect and engaged in a massive lobbying effort to keep Congress from voting to disapprove the regulation or amend the law on which the regulation was based.

Congress Considers Disapproving Final Regulation

Resolutions to disapprove the Title IX regulation partially or totally were introduced in June 1975 in both the House and the Senate. Representative James O'Hara (D., Mich.), who chaired the House Postsecondary Education Subcommittee, held several days of hearings to obtain the views of education, athletic, student, and women's groups on whether Congress should disapprove the final regulation. The major concern expressed at these hearings related to the impact of the regulation on intercollegiate sports. The National Collegiate Athletic Association and college football coaches forcefully, if not always convincingly, presented their view that the regulation would end or seriously weaken athletic programs in football and basketball. It became clear at these hearings that congressional action on the Title IX regulation would not be decided based on the narrow issue of whether the regulation was consistent with the law. The groups and members of Congress opposing the regulation were actually expressing their opposition to the requirements imposed by the law itself.

Shortly after the conclusion of the hearings, O'Hara indicated to the members of the subcommittee that he would introduce a resolution disapproving the regulation and would hold a subcommittee meeting vote on it in the near future. As soon as the women's groups learned of O'Hara's intentions, they began contacting subcommittee members and their staffs and urging them to reject O'Hara's resolution. However, their efforts were limited by the time constraints involved and by the fact that they did not know exactly what O'Hara's resolution would contain.

Late in the day on July 7, O'Hara finally announced his plans to introduce two proposals for his subcommittee to consider the following day. One proposal was a resolution to disapprove certain parts of the regulation and to direct DHEW to rewrite the regulation without these provisions. Specifically, O'Hara had selected to oppose three provisions that were strongly supported by women's groups: the requirement that state and local education agencies engage in a self-evaluation of their policies to identify sex bias; that schools designate an employee to coordinate compliance efforts; and that schools establish an internal grievance procedure for resolving sex discrimination complaints. O'Hara contended that these three provisions, while possibly worthwhile activities, went beyond the rule-making authority granted to DHEW by Congress when it passed Title IX. O'Hara also announced his intention to submit an NCAA endorsed proposal as an amendment to Title IX that would allow sports to use their profits to support their own activities before having these profits used to support other men's and women's teams. This amendment would also allow sex-segregated physical education classes to continue to exist. O'Hara placed the sports and athletic provisions into an amendment, rather than in the disapproving resolution, because he believed Congress had not provided clear guidance on these topics when it had originally passed Title IX, thus leaving DHEW free to write the regulation as it did.

On the morning of July 8, O'Hara called a meeting of his Postsecondary Education Subcommittee to consider his proposals, even though he had not even had the time to officially introduce them in the House since it had not reconvened from its Independence Day recess. In a matter of hours, the subcommittee, bowing to pressure from O'Hara and the NCAA, superficially considered and then voted to approve both of O'Hara's proposals. The subcommittee took these actions in spite of protests from several subcommittee members that the subcommittee should not vote on either proposal since they had not formally been introduced. Other members of the subcommittee complained about being forced to vote on an amendment on which no hearings had ever been held.[e] Despite these protests, the subcommittee voted 11-7 to

---

[e]The hearings the subcommittee had held on Title IX focused entirely on whether the regulation had gone beyond the law passed by Congress and did not consider at all the implications of the amendment O'Hara was now sponsoring.

approve the resolution and 12-6 to approve the amendment. After ramming the proposals through the subcommittee, O'Hara announced that Representative Carl Perkins (D., Ky.), who chaired the full Education and Labor Committee, had agreed to hold an emergency meeting of the committee the next morning to vote on the resolution and the bill.

The remainder of that day and into the night representatives from women's groups frantically tried to contact Education and Labor Committee members and their staffs to urge them to vote against O'Hara's proposals. However, even as they went about making contacts, there was a general mood of pessimism as the women feared O'Hara would be able to push the proposals through the Committee as had been done with the subcommittee.

On July 9, the Education and Labor Committee met to consider the proposals. At this time, several senior Democrats on the Committee strenuously objected to the speed and manner with which the Committee was acting. However, Committee chair Perkins ruled against all moves to delay Committee consideration of the proposals. Representative Augustus Hawkins (D., Calif.) admonished the proposal's supporters for the "rah-rah, let's go-out-for-the-college-team" attitude with which the proposals were being presented and urged the rest of the Committee members not to act on the proposals as if they were taking part in a fraternity prank. Hawkins then introduced a motion to send the resolution, which also came under the jurisdiction of the Equal Opportunities Subcommittee that he chaired, to his Subcommittee for further study. O'Hara responded by arguing that such a move would in effect kill the resolution since the Title IX regulation was scheduled to go into effect in less than two weeks. Surprisingly, Hawkin's motion was passed by a close 21-18 vote.

O'Hara next asked the Committee to consider his athletics amendment, which had been heavily lobbied for by the NCAA. However, the Committee never directly voted on the bill, but instead voted 30-8 to send the bill back to O'Hara's subcommittee for hearings. Obviously angered at the thought of holding more hearings, O'Hara protested to the Committee that he had already "wasted" ten days holding hearings on the "whole damnable subject" and complained that there was nothing more to be learned from requiring him to hold additional hearings.

The defeat of O'Hara's proposals came as a surprise to the women's groups. Although they had come within two votes of losing on the resolution to disapprove the regulation, the women's groups in the end had been able to forestall any weakening of the Title IX law or regulation. The women's groups were greatly aided in their efforts by women staff members in the House, who worked extremely hard and made extensive use of their contacts and influence to defeat the proposals. Without the support and assistance of these feminist staffers, it is unlikely that the women's groups could have turned back both proposals.

On July 14, after hearing statements from O'Hara and from DHEW,

Hawkins' subcommittee voted unanimously against O'Hara's resolution to disapprove the regulation. With the rejection of the resolution by the Equal Opportunities Subcommittee, the threat that Congress would keep the Title IX regulation from going into effect ended, since the Senate Labor and Welfare Subcommittee had voted not to even consider the resolution to disapprove the regulation that had been introduced in the Senate. As a result, on July 21, three years after the law containing Title IX had gone into effect, the regulation to implement that law became effective.

More Amendments to Title IX Considered by Congress

While the fate of the O'Hara proposals was being decided by the House, a House-Senate Conference Committee was working on the 1976 education appropriations bill. While the Conference Committee was able to work out resolutions to all the other issues before them, they could not agree on the disposition of the Casey proposal, which had been passed by the House back in April. Stalemated, the conferees decided to send the amendment back to the House and Senate for a special vote. With less than a week in which to work before the House and Senate were scheduled to take up the issue, the coalition of women's groups that had been working on Title IX attempted to organize their most extensive lobbying effort to date on any congressional issue. Coordinating their efforts closely, the representatives from the various women's groups worked hard to contact and air their views to as many members of Congress and their staffs as possible. Hundreds of volunteers worked under the guidance of the regular representatives of such organizations as Women's Lobby, League of Women Voters, American Association of University Women, National Organization for Women, and Women's Equity Action League in a low-keyed effort that was geared more to getting the facts across than to applying any pressure. Joining in the effort were several women House members and women staff members who worked at persuading House members on the issue. In spite of this effort, which was one of the heaviest lobbying efforts ever made to influence a House vote on a single issue, the House voted on July 16 to continue supporting the Casey amendment. However, the amendment, which had originally passed by a 108 vote margin, now barely went through by a 212-211 margin.

The lobbying effort of the women's coalition proved to be more successful in influencing the Senate where on the following day the Senate voted 65-29 to reject the amendment. With the issue now back in the House, the Democratic leadership became anxious to avoid any further delays in getting the appropriations bill passed and to the President for action. Realizing that the Senate would not give in on the issue, the Democratic leadership swung its weight behind a move to strike the Casey amendment from the appropriations bill. As a result of the pressure from the leadership, the House finally relented and voted on July 18 by a 215-178 margin to delete the Casey proposal from the bill. As such, in the end it was not the pressure of the women's groups that brought defeat to the Casey amendment in the House, but the power of the Democratic party leadership and their concern for getting the appropriations bill passed quickly so that Congress would have time to override the expected presidential veto.

In view of the pressure from the women's coalition and the Democratic leadership, it is not surprising that the Casey amendment finally was defeated, but it is somewhat surprising how much support the amendment retained in spite of all the pressures to delete it. Part of the explanation for the continued support for the amendment undoubtedly rests on the generally amateurish lobbying efforts made by the women's groups. While the lobbying efforts made by the women's groups were impressive in terms of the number of women involved and the dawn-to-dusk activities they engaged in, the people involved were mostly without any previous lobbying experience. However, the women were helped in their lobbying effort by the fact that there was no organized support for the Casey proposal, since it did not involve issues with which the NCAA or any other organization was concerned. The poor drafting of the bill itself also made it easier for them to develop opposition to it. Still, the overall impact of the lobbying effort made by the coalition of women's groups in the House must have been disappointing to them. The crisis situation of having to lobby the full House and Senate at the same time tested the ability and strength of the newly developed coalition of women's groups—a test that showed how far the women had come in terms of being able to influence congressional action as well as how much further they needed to go before their impact would equal that of other major lobbying groups.

After the defeat of the Casey amendment, attempts to weaken Title IX were to continue in Congress. For example, Senator Tower introduced an amendment, which was similar to the one he had introduced and had passed by the Senate in 1974, to exempt revenue-producing sports from coverage under Title IX. Although the Senate Subcommittee on Education held hearings on the proposal, it would never be brought up for subcommittee consideration. However, in October 1976 Congress did pass several amendments to Title IX. One amendment allows scholarships to be awarded as prizes for beauty contests, while another allows Boys' State and Girls' State programs and father-son and mother-daughter events to continue to be sponsored by the schools. As the implications of complying with the regulation become clearer, additional amendments can be expected to be introduced in Congress to limit and restrict in other ways the impact of the regulation.

OCR Proceeds to Implement the Regulation

When the final regulation implementing Title IX went into effect at the end of July 1975, the Office for Civil Rights had to face the task of enforcing a regulation that had come under heavy attack from Congress, special interest groups, and a large segment of the public. To aid in the enforcement effort, one of the first actions OCR was to take was the development of a more detailed explanation of what the regulation required on the most controversial section: school and college athletic programs. After a July meeting with several football coaches, including the coach at his alma mater the University of Michigan, President Ford expressed publicly that he believed that the Title IX law might need to be amended in terms of its requirements in the sports area. The President also privately ordered DHEW to develop a better and more specific explanation of what Title IX required in the sports area so that it would not be misinterpreted.

The women's groups, when they first learned that DHEW was preparing a memorandum on the sports issue, feared that DHEW was being forced to back down because of pressure and would issue a memorandum substantially weakening the requirements contained in the final regulation. A draft of the memo being prepared by OCR, which was leaked to the women's groups, confirmed their fears. The draft memo was, from their perspective, poorly and confusingly written and generally harmful in impact. The women's groups quickly asked for and received a meeting with OCR staff members, and at this meeting, the representatives of the women groups suggested ways OCR could improve the memorandum. As a result of this input, the final version of the memorandum that OCR sent to all school and college administrators at the end of September 1975 was less objectionable to the women's groups than had been the earlier draft. Even so, there were still numerous aspects of the memorandum that disturbed some women's groups. In particular, they were upset by the fact that the memorandum provided greater clarity about areas where unequal treatment for women would be allowed. Although many of the women's groups were opposed to the content of the memorandum, they did not protest against its issuance since they realized there was nothing more they could do to change DHEW's policy.

On September 29 DHEW's new Secretary, David Mathews, announced that the Department would reopen the public comment period on the controversial proposed regulation on civil rights enforcement procedures. Mathews, who appeared more open and conciliatory towards external groups than Weinberger had, seemed unhappy with the high-handed approach DHEW had taken in secretly developing the proposed regulation. As a southerner who was previously a college administrator, Mathews would not have wanted one of his first actions at DHEW to be the issuing of a final civil rights enforcement plan vehemently opposed by civil rights and women's groups. By reopening the comment period, Mathews gave himself more time to become acquainted with the problem and alternative solutions.

In October, the OCR regional office in Dallas began sending out letters to all women as well as Mexican-Americans and handicapped persons who had filed complaints of discrimination in the five southwestern states to indicate that their grievances would not be processed because court-ordered enforcement of race discrimination complaints was consuming all of the staff's time. Women who wanted alleged violations of Title IX investigated were told by OCR that "priorities necessitated by the Federal District Court . . . made it impossible to schedule Title IX complaints at this time. Your letter will be filed until such time that our workload will allow us to process it." In effect, women were told that a law that had gone unenforced by OCR for three years because of the absence of a regulation would now continue to be unenforced, this time because OCR was too busy in other areas. As could be expected, the reaction of women's groups, as well as other groups affected by the Dallas office's action, was disbelief followed by fury and frustration. The groups saw this as just one more effort, along with the proposed consolidated enforcement procedure, the DHEW to abandon completely its legal obligation to investigate all civil rights complaints. Unable to influence DHEW officials to change the Dallas OCR office's new policy, the women's groups, as well as Spanish-speaking groups, considered taking DHEW to court to have Title IX enforced in the Dallas region.

At the same time that the Dallas OCR office announced that it would not enforce Title IX, Brigham Young University announced that it disputed the legality and constitutionality of Title IX. The university publicly stated its intention to ignore the regulation where it interfered with the teaching of what the Mormon school considered high moral principles. The university refused to follow the procedure contained in Title IX that required it to submit a written explanation of how the rules infringed on their religious beliefs in order to be exempted from coverage. The university stated that it did not mind giving its position, but that it rejected the procedure because it would "allow a bureaucrat in Washington to decide if we are sincere."[13]

The following month, Hillsdale College, a small private college known to few people outside Michigan, also announced it would not comply with Title IX because it believed that compliance would turn over control of the college to "social engineers in Washington."[14] Women's groups immediately called upon DHEW to indicate it would not tolerate the Title IX regulation's being openly defied and asked DHEW to take immediate action against these two colleges. However, DHEW made no public response and took no immediate action, thereby giving the impression that the regulation could be openly and flagrantly flouted with no repercussions.[f]

In November, while DHEW was refusing to take action against Brigham Young or Hillsdale, Secretary Mathews was embarassed by the public disclosure that he had refused to even meet with the representatives of seventeen groups, concerned with the rights of women who represented over one million members, to discuss enforcement of Title IX and other sex discrimination issues.[15] Following the unfavorable publicity resulting from this disclosure, Mathews

---

[f]Five months later, in March 1976, OCR responded by inviting the two colleges to meet with OCR officials to discuss their reasons for not complying.

changed his mind and agreed to meet with these groups as well as to schedule a meeting with other civil rights groups. Prior to these meetings, fifty-seven groups concerned with civil rights and women's rights wrote Mathews urging him to take immediate action to restore public confidence in DHEW's commitment to enforce antidiscrimination laws and to correct the persistent and continuing failure of DHEW to protect the rights of minorities and women. Mathews was also told in this letter, which received national media attention, that OCR's enforcement strategy was bankrupt and that OCR and DHEW officials had no credibility among those suffering discrimination. However, the meeting between Mathews and the women's groups, when it was finally held in December 1975, produced no commitment for any changes in DHEW's handling of sex discrimination matters, to the frustration of the women attending the meeting.

In January, following the unproductive meeting with Mathews, the Women's Equity Action League joined with several other groups to file a motion in the U.S. district court asking for a preliminary injunction to stop OCR's Dallas regional office from refusing to accept sex discrimination complaints. The motion was made part of the larger lawsuit that had been pending since November 1974, which the women's groups had brought against DHEW for not adequately enforcing anti-sex discrimination laws in general. Therefore, the request for the injunction had no immediate impact on how DHEW implemented, or did not implement, Title IX.

Soon after the women's groups went to court to force DHEW to enforce Title IX, DHEW was subjected to another lawsuit, however, this one was aimed at keeping DHEW from enforcing the regulation in regard to intercollegiate athletics. In February, the NCAA filed a suit in U.S. district court in Kansas City against DHEW to challenge the validity of the provisions in Title IX concerning intercollegiate sports. The NCAA suit asked for an injunction to keep DHEW from enforcing the parts of the regulation dealing with sports and asked for a declaratory judgment that the regulation was unlawful and unconstitutional in that it went beyond the law and the intent of Congress.

In February, DHEW was to go to court itself in hope of getting released from a court-imposed requirement on how it investigated race discrimination complaints. DHEW filed a motion requesting that the U.S. district court in Washington consider modifying the timetable it had imposed on the Department in March 1975 requiring OCR to promptly process complaints of race discrimination in seventeen southern and border states. DHEW argued that it had to reassign staff members and delay or drop other civil rights enforcement activities in order to meet the court ordered timetable. Specifically, OCR argued that it could not enforce sex bias and national origin bias complaints adequately as long as it was under court order regarding the processing of race discrimination complaints. DHEW asked the court to allow it to investigate only one-quarter of the complaints filed in the race area, thus freeing its staff to also investigate one-quarter of the complaints filed under Title IX. Women's groups immediately attacked the plan DHEW proposed and insisted that DHEW should be required to meet its full legal obligation to investigate all Title IX complaints.

Toward the end of March, Secretary Mathews announced that he would not put into effect the controversial regulation on the procedures to be used in investigating civil rights complaints that had originally been proposed the preceeding June. Mathews rejected the regulation because he did not want DHEW to push through an enforcement approach that was opposed by every civil rights group in the country as well as by a substantial number of Senators and Representatives. Mathews, who had established as one of his major goals as Secretary the opening up of the bureaucratic decision-making process to outside groups, did not follow through with a plan developed in secrecy before he had come to DHEW. Instead, Mathews indicated that the Department would continue, as best it could, to meet its obligation to investigate individual complaints filed with DHEW. However, he pointed out that the Department simply did not have the staff to investigate all complaints and already had a substantial backlog of cases.[g] Mathews invited the public and civil rights groups to provide HEW with suggestions on how it should solve the dilemma resulting from not having a staff large enough to investigate all the civil rights complaints filed with the Department.

While the women and civil rights groups had won a victory in getting DHEW to drop for the time being its proposed consolidated procedures regulation, the end result was that they had just managed to maintain the unsatisfactory status quo where DHEW inadequately enforced civil rights laws. In addition, there was no assurance that the procedures eventually developed by the Department, after having received public input on the issue, would be any more satisfactory than the proposed regulation that DHEW had decided not to adopt.

While the process of determining how DHEW should enforce Title IX was argued in the courts, debated in Congress, and analyzed internally by DHEW, schools and colleges were expected to begin the process of changing their policies and practices to bring them into compliance with the regulation. In addition, the regulation required education institutions to take a number of administrative actions: appoint a Title IX enforcement coordinator; notify all students and employees that it did not discriminate on the basis of sex; start reviewing its programs and policies for sex discrimination; and begin developing a grievance procedure for resolving sex discrimination complaints.

One year after the regulation went into effect there was little hard evidence available on which to judge the extent of compliance by local schools and

---

[g]Three months later, in order to resolve suits against the Department, DHEW agreed to the demands of women's and other civil rights groups that it eliminate the backlog of elementary and secondary school complaints and promptly investigate all new complaints. The agreement was accepted and made a formal court order by the U.S. district court in Washington where the suits against DHEW had been filed. However, DHEW continued to expect a substantial backlog of higher education complaints and not investigate promptly new complaints concerning colleges.

colleges. OCR appeared not to want to know what the amount of compliance was, and women's groups were unable to compile the nationwide data needed to make this type of assessment. However, both DHEW officials and women's groups leaders agreed that it was unlikely that any school district or college was in complete compliance with all the regulation's requirements. Outright opposition to implementing the regulation was voiced by a number of school and college officials, and even some of the most inoffensive and nonthreatening procedural requirements, such as naming a Title IX coordinator, were ignored by some schools and colleges. However, the main reaction of most schools and colleges appeared to be a slow, tentative movement to make the minimum amount of effort so as not to be blatantly in noncompliance with the regulation. Clearly, there was little enthusiasm in the education community for the regulation and even less acceptance of the regulation's requirements as long overdue reforms in the way schools and colleges treated women students and faculty.

There clearly was a need during the first year of enforcing Title IX for OCR to take several actions, including: undertaking a massive informational campaign to explain the regulation's meaning; providing extensive technical assistance to schools and colleges that were in the process of reviewing their policies, and initiating numerous compliance reviews to determine the extent to which the regulation was being obeyed. However, OCR made only a minimal and generally ineffective effort to get the implementation effort off to a good start. The staff of the ten regional offices of OCR had inadequate training in enforcing Title IX and had received ambiguous guidance from the central office in Washington on policy questions. As a result, regional offices frequently gave out conflicting advice to schools and colleges on the policies required by Title IX. Rulings made by the regional offices and national OCR headquarters on the legality of school policies, and interpretations made of the meaning of the regulation, were not collected in any central file or shared between offices. The result was even more confusion than would normally be the case when enforcing a regulation for the first time. In addition, the advice given by OCR Regional Offices to schools on the legality of specific practices was not always backed up by headquarters as in the case of the schools continuing to participate in the American Legion-sponsored Girls' and Boys' State programs. In one instance that involved father-son and mother-daughter activities engaged in by schools, both the President and the Secretary of DHEW publicly criticized a regional office's policy interpretation prohibiting such activities.[16] As a result, the effectiveness of the OCR regional offices in bringing about compliance with Title IX was diminished even more.

During much of the first year of Title IX enforcement, OCR was without a permanent director and was in general disarray due to impending plans for a massive internal office reorganization. Because of these factors, combined with the already overwhelming case load from other civil rights laws, OCR was able to investigate and resolve few Title IX complaints. As a result, six years after the initial legislative proposal that became Title IX was introduced in Congress, the achievement of equality for women in education remained an unreached goal. Female students who were sophomores in high school when the proposal for an anti-sex discrimination law was first presented to Congress had graduated from college never having benefited from the legal requirement that they be treated in a nondiscriminatory manner. Changes and reforms in the way women students and faculty were treated were being made, often for the first time, but the progress appeared to be glacially slow considering the amount of time schools and colleges had to prepare to make the required changes.

Concluding Observations

When Congress passed Title IX in 1972, it was voting for a general principle of equality; the specific implications of the law were understood by few members of Congress. While considering Bayh's and Green's proposals, Congress was primarily concerned with the question of exempting from coverage particular types of schools and certain policies. Congress made no attempt to provide a clear and complete definition of what constituted sex discrimination in education. As a result, the real public debate on the issues involved in eliminating sex discrimination followed, rather than proceeded, the passage of the law.

It was only years later, after DHEW had drafted the regulation to implement the law, that Congress finally came to understand what Title IX actually meant in terms of changes in educational policies and practices. When the implications became known, many members of Congress realized that they disagreed with the impact of the law for which they had previously voted. As a result, Title IX has been under almost constant assault in both the House and the Senate. In all probability, attempts to change the law will continue in the future, especially through last minute introduction of amendments to other education bills. This tactic will make it extremely difficult for women's groups to organize and defeat the amendments, and therefore, weakening amendments may very well be approved by one House. However, the women's coalition seems strong enough at this point to be able to turn back most amendments once they have the opportunity to lobby, especially since there is usually no organized interests on the opposite side of the issue.

It is difficult to fully explain congressional reaction to Title IX. The topic of sex discrimination is a highly emotional one, the issues involved go to the root of societal sex roles, on which most of the male members of Congress remain extremely traditional in outlook. In addition, many of the issues, particularly sports and athletics, have sexual overtones. The thought of adolescent girls and boys playing sports together is something that many in Congress simply cannot accept. The issue of sex discrimination in general, and sports in particular, brings out expressions of the personal value systems of the members of Congress. As a result, it has been difficult to predict who will support and who will oppose efforts to weaken Title IX. The normal support on civil right issues usually provided by liberal Democrats is not assured on sex discrimination issues. The position of the members of Congress appears to be more related to personal and family factors than to political ideology, although the bulk of support for Title IX still comes from moderate and liberal Democrats.

Not only has Title IX tapped some very deep congressional feelings regarding proper roles for men and women in society, but it has also brought out strong emotions on the proper role of the federal government in setting local educational policy. Many of the members of Congress who have opposed Title IX have done so because of their belief that the federal government should not be so deeply involved in local educational matters. If the belief that the federal government has gone too far in regulating local educational policies grows, as can be expected, so will the opposition to Title IX.

A byproduct of the congressional battles over Title IX has been the emergence of a strong women's lobby on sex discrimination issues. The creation of a formal National Coalition for Women and Girls in Education with representatives from forty groups can be directly attributed to Title IX. Although this coalition has shown itself to be quite effective, there is a real danger that it will not be able to use its influence on new and different issues. Instead, it may be constantly using its legislative lobbying efforts to defend the basic Title IX law passed in 1972. As such, it may be difficult for these groups to have the major impact it would like to have on other social, economic, and education legislative issues of concern to women or to spend as much time as it would like attempting to get the executive branch to enforce antidiscrimination requirements.

The performance of DHEW and its Office for Civil Rights in the development and implementation of Title IX has been deficient from a number of perspectives. The two years it took to develop the proposed regulation was inexcusably long. An internal DHEW management system that provided inadequate oversight over OCR, combined with poor administration and the lack of strong leadership in OCR itself contributed to the slow speed at which the regulation was developed. Considering the chaotic state of OCR during most of this time period, it is not surprising that it took such a long time to issue a proposed regulation; it is a wonder that a regulation got developed at all.

The process used in developing the regulation and the decisions made on the content of the regulation were mainly a product of the management style and personal philosophy of Secretary Weinberger. In fact, Weinberger believed that the Title IX regulation was among the major accomplishments of his tenure at DHEW and always displayed a strong interest in the topic, to the extent that his immediate staff was sometimes annoyed with him because he would spend so much time on it and not on other matters awaiting his attention. Weinberger was decisive in his actions on the issue; once he made up his mind he could not be swayed by staff positions. In fact, it frequently appeared that he had already made up his mind on a subject and did not even bother to read the material on the issue prepared for him by his staff. Undoubtedly due to his personal and political philosophy, Weinberger selected the weakest option on almost every issue with the major exception of the issue of how to cover profit-making sports. Although the wisdom of his decisions on the issues can be disputed, for the most part the policies he selected were at least legally supportable. However, there are a number of important exceptions. For example, the legality of Weinberger's decisions not to cover the admissions policies of private undergraduate professional schools and not to cover textbooks and curricula materials in the regulation can be questioned, and his decision not to cover Rhodes scholarships appears to have been without legal merit.

In general, it appears that Weinberger was unwilling to require policies that would rapidly move the country away from traditional sex-role patterns. However, he did exhibit a strong belief that women should be treated better by the education system and was insistent that the regulation achieve at least this objective.

The manner in which OCR is implementing Title IX reflects the reality of a general political climate that is hostile toward federal government intervention in local education matters. In addition, support for government action in behalf of the civil rights of minorities is also on the wane and opposition to the demands of women's rights advocates have become more pronounced. As a result, OCR has not forcefully required schools to comply with Title IX. The staff of OCR is personally committed to eliminating sex bias in education, and given a different political climate and greater support from the President and Secretary, could launch a major enforcement effort. However, the heavy demands placed on OCR by its various civil rights responsibilities means that the attention paid to Title IX will in the future, probably continue to be inadequate to meet the demands of enforcement. What OCR could do instead is strictly and comprehensively enforce Title IX in a selected number of school districts and colleges and highly publicize these enforcement activities, thus creating an enforcement climate that encourages voluntary compliance out of fear of the consequence of being found in noncompliance. Until such an atmosphere is created, Title IX will remain largely a rhetorical statement of what women's rights in education should be, rather than a legal statement of the obligations schools and colleges have to their women students and employees.

Notes

Except where otherwise footnoted, the information presented in this chapter was obtained from interviews with persons listed below and documents provided by them. Also indicated is the capacity in which these people were interviewed.

Of necessity, the material presented in the chapter relies on the authors' interpretation of the information obtained from these sources.

Interview with Bernice Sandler, former staff member of the House Special Subcommittee on Education and current Director of the Project on the Status and Education of Women, Association of American Colleges, February 1975.

Interview with Carol Burris, Director of Women's Lobby, Inc., February 1975.

Interview with Holly Knox, former special Assistant to the Assistant Secretary for Education, Department of Health, Education and Welfare and current Director of the Project on Equal Education Rights, NOW Legal Defense and Education Fund, February 1975.

Interview with B. Ann Kliendienst, former Director of the Women's Action Program, Department of Health, Education and Welfare and current Director of the Office of Special Concerns, Department of Health, Education and Welfare, February 1975.

Interview with Alexandra Buek, Office of the General Counsel, Department of Health, Education and Welfare, March 1975.

Interview with Gwen Gregory, Director of the Office of Policy Communication, Office of Civil Rights, Department of Health, Education and Welfare, February 1975.

1. U.S. House of Representatives, *Hearings before the House Special Subcommittee on Education, Committee on Education and Labor on Discrimination Against Women*, 91st Congress, 2nd Session, Washington, D.C., 1970.

2. For the full text of the debate, see 117 *Congressional Record* 30399-415, August 6, 1971.

3. *House of Representatives Report*, No. 92-1085, 92nd Congress, 2nd Session.

4. For the full text of the debate, see 117 *Congressional Record* 39248-63, November 4, 1971.

5. 117 *Congressional Record* 43080-1, November 4, 1971.

6. 118 *Congressional Record* 5804, February 28, 1972.

7. Ibid., p. 5807.

8. Ibid., p. 5813.

9. For the full text of the questions and answers at this session, see U.S. Department of Health, Education and Welfare, Transcript of Press Briefing Held by Secretary Caspar Weinberger on June 18, 1974.

10. *HEW News*, July 8, 1974.

11. For a full analysis of the positions taken in the comments submitted on Title IX, see, Andrew Fishel, "Organizational Positions on Title IX: Conflicting Perspectives on Sex Discrimination on Edcuation," *Journal of Higher Education* XLVII (January-February 1976), pp. 93-105.

12. *Federal Register*, June 4, 1975.

13. "Brigham Young University Challenges Part of Bias Law," *Chronicle of Higher Education*, October 28, 1975, p. 1.

14. "Hillsdale Won't Comply," *Chronicle of Higher Education*, November 3, 1975, p. 6.

15. Nancy Hicks, "H.E.W. Chief Declines to Discuss Sex Bias With Women's Groups," *New York Times*, November 3, 1975.

16. Bart Barnes, "Ford Acts to Permit Schools to Hold Father-Son Events," *Washington Post*, July 18, 1976.

6

Sex Discrimination in Education and the National Political Process

Sex discrimination in education emerged as a national political issue for the first time in 1970. The major events that have transpired since then—the Cohen vs. Chesterfield County maternity leave case, the Office of Education's task force on women's education, the Women's Educational Equity Act, and Title IX—constitute a significant portion of the total involvement of the legislative, executive, and judicial branches of the federal government regarding the question of sex discrimination in education in the 1970s. Accordingly, it is possible to draw from these four case histories some initial conclusions regarding the nature of the politics involved in challenging the existence of sex discrimination in education. Specifically, viewing the roles and behaviors of each of the three branches of government in this cross-case perspective provides a framework for identifying those factors that have acted to inhibit change as well as those factors that have acted to facilitate the elimination of sex-biased practices and policies. This cross-case approach also allows for an assessment to be made of the involvement and performance of national organizations on issues relating to sex discrimination in education.

The Legislative Branch

The most striking aspect of congressional behavior concerning women in education has been the superficiality of the interest expressed by most members of Congress. Over the years only a handful of Senators and Representatives have invested significant time or energy in working either for or against proposals relating to women in education. Because there has been no substantial or continuing interest in the area, the level of knowledge and understanding possessed by most members of Congress has been minimal. As a result, women's rights groups have had to expend a great amount of time and energy just to obtain the initial attention of congressional members and then to educate them on this topic.

Educational and informational lobbying campaigns have been, by necessity, the primary approach taken by the women's rights groups when attempting to influence Congress. This approach has been one to which the women's groups are well-suited due to the particular background and skills of the leaders. Most members of Congress have reacted favorably to this lobbying style. However, this approach not only places a great burden on the women's groups to present

137

extensive legal and social science documentation to support their positions but leaves them vulnerable when more aggressive tactics are utilized by opposing interest groups.

Even when massive evidence has been presented to show the different treatment afforded men and women students and faculty, the reaction of members of Congress has not always been sympathetic to the plight of the women. The hostility of most Republicans and Southern Democrats to women's rights in general has been the dominant pattern affecting the education area as well. In addition, a significant number of Democrats who are otherwise supportive of liberal and civil rights causes have been either inactive or nonsupportive in the area of women's educational rights. The personal beliefs of members of Congress on appropriate sex-role behavior, rather than their general political stance or position on other civil rights issues, seems to be the most important factor in determining the actions and positions taken on sex discrimination issues.

It has only been due to the adept performance of the members of Congress who have assumed leadership in the effort to achieve equity for women in education that legislative success in this area has resulted. Although recently the growing number of women in the House has strengthened the hand of women's rights advocates, during the early 1970s, there were few women in the House to champion the cause of women's rights, and none, or only a couple, in the Senate. Without the efforts of a handful of members of Congress—such as Mink, Mondale, Bayh, and, initially, Green—women would not have had any leaders in Congress to represent and fight for their interests. These congressional advocates have made skillful use of hearings on sexism in education in order to create a climate—at the subcommittee and committee levels and in Congress in general— that was favorable towards considering legislation on women in education. The hearings have also been effectively used to help publicize and legitimatize criticisms of the education system for being sex biased, thereby creating public interest and support for legislation in this area.

By making use of their positions on key subcommittees and committees, as well as by utilizing their presence on House-Senate Conference Committees, these few Senators and Representatives have often been able to sway the outcome on the consideration of a women's bill even though these women and men are not among the most influential members of Congress. To a large degree, the success enjoyed by the congressional advocates of women's educational rights can be attributed to the fact that they have been far more interested in the issues and more inclined to fight much harder than their opponents. It is no coincidence that a large number of the most involved individuals in the House have been women Representatives.

Since these few Representatives and Senators have been willing to extend themselves on these issues, raising objections has been much less attractive to opponents with only limited interest in the issues. Although the issues under consideration sometimes affect a particular interest group, more often there is no organized constituency opposing the women's rights advocates. This lack of organized resistance results in fewer incentives for congressional members, who would ordinarily be ideologically inclined to press for positions antagonistic to women's rights, to actually do so. As such, it is not surprising that few in Congress have felt strongly enough to become heavily involved in opposing legislation concerning women's equality in education.

However, since few Representatives or Senators have been deeply interested or knowledgeable on this topic, they have frequently been easily swayed by appeals to emotion and have reacted in response to sensational claims. The nature of the issues involved (such as fraternities and sororities, youth organizations, coeducational physical education, sports teams, and beauty contests) have encouraged appeals to emotion and the use of scare tactics. In addition, the nature of these topics has sometimes resulted in superficial treatment of the topics, even though policies regarding athletics and social activities have a substantial impact on the education of women.

Although professional women staff members are a distinct minority in Congress and generally are found in lower level positions than male staff members, many women employees in both congressional and committee offices have taken an intense interest in sexism in education. These women have used their intimate knowledge of the legislative process to initiate the use of procedures that are favorable to the consideration of sexism issues and have used their personal contacts and influence to affect the outcome. Without the interest of and assistance from these staff members, the efforts to achieve legislative gains for women in education would not have been as successful.

As has been the case with members of Congress, most staff members who are not supportive of the goals sought by the women's groups have been unwilling to devote much time or energy on the issue. As a general rule, male staff members, because they are less directly concerned and interested in sex discrimination and because their higher staff positions give them numerous other legislative responsibilities, have generally not been heavily involved on women's issues. In contrast, the outcome of legislation concerning women has served as a major opportunity and challenge to the female staff members to influence the outcome on a topic of personal importance to them.

The alliance of members of Congress, congressional staff members, and women's organizations working intensively on legislation relating to sexism in education has created a formidable obstacle to their opponents. In response, their adversaries have generally made use of parliamentary tactics to achieve their goals, rather than direct votes on the merits of the issues involved. The use of parliamentary tactics, combined with the submission of amendments at the last minute without any previous publicity, have been approaches that have sometimes been successful. However, the women's groups have generally been able to keep such ploys from achieving final success, most often by relying on one house to rectify the actions of the other house. Senate committees, in particular, have often been unwilling to go along with hastily approved actions by the House. Still, this approach of introducing floor amendments without previous hearings has set the tone for congressional consideration of women in education questions.

The topic of sexual equality in education has generally been considered a peripheral side issue to broader and more important legislation under consideration, especially appropriation bills for DHEW programs and omnibus education amendments. This approach has worked both to the advantage and disadvantage of the interests of women. It has helped achieve success for women by keeping the major focus of attention of most members of Congress and interest groups on other portions of the legislation being considered. Since they are limited in the number of topics that they can concentrate on at one time, the attention given to sex discrimination issues has been low in comparison to other broader issues that have more visible impact on the education programs in the home states or districts of the members of Congress. Provisions favorable to women in education have, as a result of this inattention, been able to slip through with little notice given to them or their eventual impact. Had Congress given closer attention to what it was approving relating to sex discrimination in education, it probably would not have been willing to go along so passively with the proposals being pushed by only a few Senators and Representatives.

The peripheral treatment of sexism issues has also served as a detriment to the achievement of action favorable to women. Because of the manner in which women issues have been raised and considered, Congress has never had to confront the issues directly and to decide whether discrimination against women in education is an area of sufficient national importance to warrant close congressional attention. As a result, women's issues have often been treated lightly and in haste by a Congress anxious to get on to other matters considered more important. The time and continuous attention that the topic warrants from Congress has been absent.

Because Congress has never come to terms with the broader question of the gravity of the issue of sex discrimination in education, special interest groups concerned with specific aspects of education policy have been able to achieve greater impact than would otherwise be the case. Organizations representing interests such as those of private colleges, fraternities and sororities, and intercollegiate sports have been able to shape and narrow the consideration of issues before Congress so that they are not presented or perceived as women's rights issues, but rather as education issues. Such tactics have allowed them to achieve their objectives without having Congress consider the relationship of the specific proposal under consideration to the larger issue of the rights of women. Of course, this approach also benefits Congress in that it allows members of Congress to bow to interest-group pressure and act unfavorably to women without admitting that they have voted to deprive women of their right to equal educational opportunity. Arguments extolling the virtues of educational diversity and decrying extensive federal involvement in local educational policy making have been used to mask the real impact and intention of congressional actions.

When Congress has acted on women's issues, it has often done so by enacting broadly stated legislation that must be more narrowly defined by the executive branch in order to be implemented. The discretion granted the President and DHEW by Congress has been substantial, and the resulting policies have not always been satisfactory to members of Congress. Congressional reluctance to legislate specific policies provides the executive branch no other choice but to make major decisions on how to operationalize what Congress has enacted. Congress has in effect relinquished its responsibility to the executive branch to resolve the most difficult and controversial issues regarding sex discrimination in education. By so doing, the liberal Democrats in Congress, who have been the primary supporters of women's rights in education, have turned over decision making to an executive branch controlled by the opposing party, which has a significantly different view than their own.

The endorsement by liberal Democrats of broadly worded legislation on sex discrimination in education can be justified on the grounds that this type of proposal was the easiest to get passed. However, once Congress had granted substantial discretion to the executive branch, the Democrats in Congress who supported the legislation should have made extensive use of their legislative oversight capabilities in order to ensure that the executive branch was implementing these laws on a timely basis and in a manner consistent with congressional intent. However, to a large extent, close monitoring of the administration's performance on sex discrimination policies has not taken place. This lack is true for those in Congress who oppose forceful enforcement of civil rights laws as well as for those who want to see strict enforcement of these requirements. For the most part, the administration has remained substantially unaccountable for its performance in this area. Since Congress by and large considers DHEW's civil rights performance as too strong, this neglect of its oversight responsibilities may end up as a fortunate consequence for women's and other civil rights groups.

The Executive Branch

The emergence of sex discrimination in education as a national issue has taken place entirely during the tenure of conservative Republican presidents. The behavior of the executive branch was obviously greatly affected by this political factor.

In the 1970-1976 time period, there has been a massive retreat in the civil rights area in general from previously expressed commitments. In the sex discrimination area, the Nixon Administration opposed the Women's Educational Equity Act and opposed the enactment of the provision that was to become Title IX. After the passage of these proposals, the administration refused to launch a major initiative against sexism in education as illustrated by its low budget request to implement the Women's Educational Equity Act and by its slow and unimpressive enforcement of Title IX. In responding to congressional initiatives, both the Nixon and Ford Administrations have shown little commitment to the achievement of significant gains for women in education. Instead, concerns over the size of federal educational expenditures and the involvement of the federal government in regulating school and college policies has dominated Republican presidential actions.

Given the lack of support from the President, it is difficult to see how the three men who have served as Secretary of DHEW during the 1970-1976 time period could have moved very aggressively against sexism in education. Still, only Elliot Richardson seems to have been personally very sympathetic to the unfair treatment received by women students and faculty. Both Caspar Weinberger, and more recently David Mathews, exhibited far more concern with the goal of keeping DHEW from being deeply involved in local educational policy making than with achieving educational equity for women. Admittedly, the social and political environment when Richardson was heading DHEW made it easier for him to be supportive of women's rights: The goals of the women's movement had not as yet come under severe criticism and public resentment of federal involvement in school affairs had not become so pronounced. Still the personal commitment displayed by Richardson in this area has not been matched by his two successors. No matter how restrained in actual behavior they might have had to be as a result of the altered political and social climate, Weinberger and Mathews could have easily provided far greater leadership if they had been ideologically so inclined.

Although Richardson was concerned about improving the status of women in education, his short tenure at DHEW and his concern for a large number of other issues prevented him from bringing about the maximum amount of change. In particular, his failure to hold the Office for Civil Rights or the Office of Education strictly accountable for implementing his women's rights objectives on a timely basis seriously detracted from his impact. Richardson's successor at DHEW also had the kind of forceful management style necessary to bring about a great amount of progress in the way the Department viewed the issue of sex discrimination. However, Weinberger lacked the philosophical commitment to use his authority to obtain major departmental action in this area. Mathews, in his short time at DHEW, lacked both the forceful management style and philosophic commitment to bring the Department's resources to focus on the issue of sexism in education.

The lesson from these three secretaries is clear: It takes personal commitment combined with a strong and forceful managerial style to move DHEW in a coordinated fashion toward the objective of educational equity for women. In the absence of either of these factors, the Office of Education and the Office for Civil Rights will be able to operate with substantial autonomy in their policies regarding sexism in education. Even if the Secretary was not personally interested, DHEW could have a more effective women's rights strategy if any of the other influential departmental officials were strongly concerned. However, this has never been the case.

The absence of women in general from the top eschelons of DHEW has resulted in the decisions on sexism issues being made almost exclusively by men. However, a number of important staff positions have been held by women who have been interested and involved in women's rights. It is due to the efforts of these women staff members that DHEW has taken as much action as it has in the area of sex bias. However, without strong leadership and commitment from the top, the full power and resources of DHEW will never be applied to eliminating sex bias in education.

The Office of Education has demonstrated no real interest in the problem of sexism. The strong and close ties held by OE officials with the various parts of the male-dominated education community has probably been largely responsible for the unaggressive performance of OE. OE officials to a large extent mirror and reflect the attitudes and biases prevalent among school and college administrators. Most persons in OE, and in leadership positions in education in general, seem to consider the issue of sex bias as an administrative nuisance to be dispensed with as quickly and painlessly as possible rather than as a serious social injustice to be rectified by immediate government action. Thus, it is not surprising that OE officials have not made the elimination of sexism a major objective and never considered it when developing policies to implement other programs. What token efforts OE has made to address the issue of sex discrimination have usually been initiated as a result of outside pressure from Congress, women's rights groups, or through the efforts of individual staff members.

At no time, however, has OE engaged in activities that threatened prevailing sexist policies and practices. Instead, OE has left all of the unpleasant, combative actions regarding eliminating sex-biased policies in schools and colleges to the Office for Civil Rights. By refusing to take on any major responsibility in the area of eliminating sex discrimination, OE has helped place the entire burden on OCR—a burden that OCR has not been able to handle.

The Office for Civil Rights has always been an office operated in the midst of controversy. By the very nature of its responsibilities, OCR is constantly involved with highly emotional and politically and legally controversial issues. Since its creation in 1967, OCR's primary responsibility has been the achievement of racial integration in schools. The constant turbulence over school desegregation and busing issues has resulted in OCR's never establishing a well-organized and smoothly functioning operation. Instead, OCR's operation moves from one crisis to another without any long-range planning or clear policy direction. OCR's unimpressive enforcement of Title VI of the 1964 Civil Rights Act during the late 1960s and early 1970s provided little reason to expect that it would be more effective in its enforcement of Title IX. Still, the slow pace at which OCR proceeded to develop the regulation to implement Title IX and the uncoordinated, half-hearted efforts it has made to enforce the regulation did not occur totally due to inefficiency. Rather, this behavior is in part symptomatic of a larger overriding philosophy guiding OCR's behavior. Top administration officials have never considered OCR's mission as being the achievement of strict and total compliance with the law of the land. Instead, OCR has spent most of its energies attempting to achieve as much compliance as possible through persuasion and informal pressure. Only when forced by political or judicial pressure has OCR made use of its full legal authority to bring about compliance with civil rights laws. Political expediency, rather than adherence to the law, has been the guiding principle of OCR's operation.

Given the fact that OCR was created initially to deal with race discrimination, it is not surprising that most of its male employees, both black and white, at first did not consider sex discrimination as a serious problem. Indeed, many viewed anti-sex discrimination requirements as harmful since they would invariably detract OCR's attention from the area of race discrimination. Although extensive training and education efforts have been undertaken, the knowledge and understanding possessed by OCR staff of what constitutes sex discrimination remains varied. Given a staff that is only newly concerned with sex discrimination and still unsure about how to define it, combined with weak and indecisive leadership in OCR and DHEW in general on civil rights, it is not surprising the OCR's performance in enforcing Title IX has been disappointing to women's rights advocates.

One consequence of OCR's poor record in resolving sex discrimination complaints has been the reluctance of women to file complaints under Title IX. At the beginning of 1976, only around four hundred complaints had been filed under Title IX concerning elementary and secondary school policies and practices, and there had been only two-hundred sixty complaints involving institutions of higher education. If female students, their parents, and women teachers expected their complaints to be investigated and resolved, there surely would have been a far greater number of complaints filed since sex discriminatory practices remain widespread. However, there is a realistic expectation on the part of aggrieved students and teachers that OCR will not provide them assistance in obtaining a fair disposition of their complaints. In fact, as of January 1976, only one-third of the small number of Title IX complaints filed had actually been resolved.

In assessing OCR's performance in enforcing Title IX, it must be realized that OCR is responsible for enforcing six other laws in addition to Title IX.[a] It is unrealistic to expect OCR's performance in enforcing Title IX to improve unless there is a total overhaul of its entire method of operation. The number of complaints filed with OCR under all of its authorities has increased so substantially that even with large staff increases it has been unable to devote the necessary staff resources to investigate the complaints. In 1969, DHEW estimates that OCR received less than 300 complaints, while during 1975 it estimates that it received seven or eight times this number. OCR staff increased by less than three times its number during this same time. The result of this imbalance can be seen in its case backlog. At the end of 1969, OCR had only fifty-eight unresolved complaints, while at the end of 1975, it had approximately 1,800 cases that still needed to be resolved.

Contributing to the overall civil rights backlog has been the growing number of sex discrimination complaints filed. The complaints filed under Title IX have increased each year in absolute numbers and in terms of the percent of all complaints filed with OCR. In 1972, the year the Title IX law was passed, complaints under this authority constituted only 2 percent of the total OCR received. In 1975, Title IX complaints constituted one-fourth of all of OCR's workload, and sex discrimination complaints under Title IX, as well as other laws, constituted almost 40 percent of all the complaints filed with OCR.

While it is possible to sympathize with the massive enforcement problems confronted by OCR, the poor start it made toward enforcing Title IX is still inexcusable. As the data on the type of complaints filed with OCR show, sex discrimination has become a major responsibility for OCR. The Title IX regulation drafted by DHEW under the careful guidance of Secretary Weinberger was moderate enough in its requirements that there was little reason for protests on the part of school and college officials. This factor, combined with the three-year grace period that schools and colleges have had to make changes in their policies and practices before OCR finalized the Title IX regulation, would seem to have justified a vigorous enforcement effort being made once the final regulation was published. The time period immediately following the effective

---

[a]Besides Title IX, OCR is responsible for enforcing Title VI of the Civil Rights Act of 1964, which prohibits discrimination based on race, color, and national origin by schools, universities, health, and welfare agencies; Sections 799A and 845 of the Public Health Service Act, which prohibits sex discrimination by medical, nursing, and other health-related schools; Section 504 of the Rehabilitation Act of 1973, which covers discrimination against the handicapped by schools and universities; Section 407 of the Drug Abuse Office and Treatment Act of 1972 and Section 321 of the Comprehensive Alcohol Abuse and Alcoholism Prevention, Treatment and Rehabilitation Act of 1970, which cover drug abusers and alcohol abusers seeking admission or treatment at private and public general hospitals; and Executive Order 11246 as amended by Executive Order 11375, which prohibits race, color, religious, sex, and national origin discrimination by educational institutions and health and welfare agencies with federal contracts. In addition, OCR will have responsibilities for enforcing the Age Discrimination Act of 1975.

date of the regulation provided a unique opportunity to bring about substantial compliance with a minimum of effort if educational institutions believed there would be a quick and strict enforcement of the regulation's requirements. Since OCR did not choose to do this, enforcement efforts will meet greater resistance from schools and colleges in succeeding years, while pressure from women's rights groups on OCR will also increase.

Therefore, OCR's initial timidity in enforcing Title IX will impede and slow down the entire process of change in the treatment of women in education. In addition, OCR's inactivity has served to create an atmosphere of confrontation rather than cooperation in the implementation of Title IX. By bowing to actual and anticipated political pressures in the first year of enforcing Title IX, OCR has intensified its already severe credibility problem, which in turn makes enforcement considerably more difficult. As has been the case in the race discrimination area for a number of years, the courts will be asked to intervene in the sex discrimination area on an increasingly frequent basis in order to achieve compliance with the law—a result that OCR has shown itself unwilling and incapable of achieving.

The Judicial Branch

The federal courts have been brought into the policy-making process relating to sex discrimination in education generally as a last resort. Individuals or organizations have sought relief from the courts only after their efforts to influence policy through the political process have failed. This can be seen in the suits filed against DHEW for not enforcing anti-sex discrimination laws, in the suit filed by the NCAA against DHEW over the impact of Title IX on intercollegiate sports, and in the case filed by Susan Cohen against the Chesterfield County school district.

In particular, the recent failure of DHEW to fulfill its legal obligation to investigate all sex discrimination complaints has placed people in the unpleasant position of either taking no action as a result of discrimination, seeking a state or local remedy, or filing suit in federal court. The expense involved in a lawsuit can be so prohibitive that very few people are able or willing to travel this route. Susan Cohen was a rare exception in that she was able to initiate her suit by finding an attorney who was willing to handle her case at no expense. Generally, people who do not have an organization's financial support cannot afford lengthy litigation, and they certainly cannot match the financial resources available to school districts and colleges to contest their cases.

Because of the expense involved in lawsuits, organizations such as the NEA DuShane Fund, Women's Equity Action League, and National Organization for Women Legal Defense and Education Fund play an important role, as does the American Civil Liberties Union whose attorneys handle precedent setting cases for free. By providing financial support for individual suits or by filing class action suits on behalf of women, these organizations perform an invaluable service. Schools, colleges, and agencies of government know that they are not immune from lawsuit for discriminatory actions against women.

The filing of a lawsuit charging sex discrimination can also act as a major public relations technique for women in that it can cause embarrassment to the school, college or agency involved. Indeed, just the threat of legal action can serve as an incentive to policymakers to deal more fairly with women in order to avoid the actual filing of a lawsuit. Even after a suit is filed, there is an incentive to resolve the suit out of court and thus keep the court from monitoring the actions of the school or government agency.

Although pro-women organizations' financial and legal resources are sometimes available to women who challenge sex-biased policies, the time involved between the filing of the suit and the final court decision can be considerable. For example, it took Susan Cohen four years to be awarded only several thousand dollars back pay for the time she was forced to take maternity leave. Thus, while court action offers the hope of eventual relief and damages, the process is often too slow to be of value to the person who files the suit. The individual student affected may no longer be attending the same school or the teacher involved may no longer be in the same job by the time the case is decided.

Making the judicial process even less attractive as a potential source for accomplishing policy change is the fact that there is never a guarantee that the legal action will be successful. Even in clear cases of discriminatory behavior, procedural errors can prevent final victory. In addition, the courts have been unwilling to elevate charges of sex discrimination to the same level as accorded to complaints of race discrimination. Policies and practices that treat women differently from men to the detriment of women may be upheld as legal by the courts if they serve a rational and legitimate state interest; issues of race must meet a much stricter judicial scrutiny. It must be emphasized that all the courts do is decide whether a particular policy is legally permissible; the courts do not decide whether it is sound or wise public policy. As a result, flawed and short-sighted policies regarding the treatment of women will not always be prevented or overturned by the courts. This is especially true considering the domination of judicial positions by males, many of whom hold traditional views on women's role in society. In addition, a political factor is involved in judicial decisions affecting sex discrimination. As exhibited in the Cohen case, at both the appellate and Supreme Court levels, all of the judges opposing Cohen had been appointed by Republican presidents. The political ideologies of judges clearly influence their views of sex discrimination cases. It is interesting to note that even in the judicial system, Republicans appear to be less sympathetic to women's rights than Democrats.

Even in the cases where the courts have decided in favor or women, the actual impact of the decisions has varied because court rulings are not self-enforcing. Noncompliance with unpopular decisions pertaining to social issues is often widespread. As a result, a favorable court decision often signals the beginning, not the end, of the battle to obtain a policy change. However, the fear of having to pay financial damages or to give back pay to women seems to be an important incentive in encouraging rapid compliance with a court decision regarding sex discrimination.

The alignment of groups involved in the Cohen case closely followed the grouping exhibited in the legislative and administrative arenas. A few women's and teachers' groups in all instances have served as the nucleus of the movement to obtain equal treatment for women. Although the national teacher organizations of NEA and AFT have been supportive of women's rights, their local affiliates have often not shared this policy perspective. As the Cohen case illustrates, the sex-biased policy that was challenged with the assistance of NEA had the support of the local education association. The dominance of local teacher organizations by male teachers has clearly contributed to this unresponsive behavior toward issues of concern to women teachers, thereby forcing women to use the judicial process rather than the collective bargaining process to achieve policy change.

One important factor differentiating the judicial process from the legislative and administrative policy-making processes is the involvement of noneducation groups. In the Cohen case, which was primarily a teachers' rights case, many groups that were involved had no interest in education policy and raised issues totally unrelated to education. It can be seen from this case that when a controversial issue with potentially broad implications reaches the Supreme Court, the scope of interested parties widens considerably. What had been, at the district and appellate court levels, a dispute between a woman teacher and her school board, eventually became a case with wide-ranging implications not only for educators but also for women's groups, labor organizations, civil liberties groups, national and state government agencies, and private businesses.

Powerful and influential organizations committed their legal staffs to produce amicus curiae briefs on both sides of the issue in the hope of influencing the court's decision. The women's and teachers' groups have shown themselves to be quite skilled at organizing and coordinating an effort aimed at influencing through the filing of briefs the court's decision regarding teachers. However, the actual impact of these efforts on the subsequent court decision is impossible to measure.

Clearly, the filing of lawsuits charging school districts and colleges with sex discrimination or charging DHEW with lack of enforcement of anti-sex discrimination laws has become an instrumental part of the overall political strategy of the groups seeking to achieve educational equity for women. In the future, the judicial branch, along with the executive and legislative branches, will be a major battleground for disputes over educational policy affecting women. The power that women generally lack in Congress and in executive departments may be partially compensated for by the courts, where the lack of political influence is not as crucial a factor in determining outcome. However, the capacity of the various interest groups to present their position, whether in the form of legal briefs or in other forms, will remain a decisive element in the struggle over policy towards women. The capabilities of the women's groups and their allies that have brought them successes in other legislative and executive areas should help them achieve victories in the courts as well.

Interest Groups

Interest-group involvement in the politics of sex discrimination in education has taken a variety of forms: the development of legislative proposals and preparation of material to support or oppose legislation under consideration; lobbying Congress on legislation; formally and informally advising and consulting with DHEW and other executive branch officials on policy issues; pressuring DHEW officials on policies towards women; filing lawsuits to end sex discrimination; and filing amicus curiae briefs in sex discrimination cases.

Most of the opposition to women's rights in education has been disorganized and sporadic. Only the NCAA has waged a coordinated effort in the courts, Congress, and executive branch in support of its position. The Council of Chief State School Officers also has made a persistent effort to get Congress and the executive branch to restrict and limit the collection of data relating to civil rights enforcement. Since the executive branch has been so unaggressive in the sex discrimination area, groups opposing women's rights have not had to make the same concerted effort to influence policy as have the women's groups and their allies that support women's progress. Another reason for the low level of activity of groups hostile to the demands of the women's groups is that often the policy issues have not been threatening to their interests. For example, the Women's Educational Equity Act, in which participation was voluntary and did not require any policy changes, went virtually unopposed. However, when policy changes are required, especially those requiring budgetary expenditures, the political alignment is quite different as can be seen on Title IX. The alignment of groups on the proposed Title IX regulation demonstrated that opposition to women's rights proposals will be extensive. Unfortunately, the voluntary corrective programs, such as the Women's Educational Equity Act, that can obtain broad political support, while useful, certainly will not be sufficient to eliminate sex bias in education. Only the strict enforcement of a law such as Title IX will accomplish this goal.

The positions that were taken by various interest groups on an issue such as the proposed Title IX regulation thus take on great significance. An analysis of the positions taken by interest groups on key issues indicated that the goals of women's groups were strongly supported by student groups and national government commissions, such as the Equal Employment Opportunity Commission and U.S. Commission on Civil Rights. Strongly opposed to the policy suggestions endorsed by women's groups were the higher education groups, college and university administrators, and state school boards associations. The Chief State School Officers and elementary and secondary education groups were generally mixed in their responses to the proposals endorsed by women's groups. This lack of unanimity in the education community on sex discrimination issues has given Congress and the executive branch substantial flexibility on how they respond to the demands of women's rights groups. When policies are decided upon that are detrimental to women's education, they can be justified and rationalized on the basis of the opposition of the educators who are actually responsible for running schools and colleges.

Because of the antagonistic position of numerous powerful education groups (especially higher education groups) and the mixed positions taken by many other groups, the burden placed on women's groups and their allies has been considerable. In response to this, and in order to work more effectively to achieve their common goals, a formal coalition has been formed of people concerned with women's education. The formation of this coalition in late 1974 and the growth in its membership and importance to the present time must be considered one of the most significant outcomes of the emergence of sex discrimination in education as a national political issue. Unwittingly, groups opposed to women's full educational equality have encouraged the development of a stronger base of support for women's lobbying efforts.

The idea for a coalition of people interested in women's education issues who worked for education and women's and civil rights organizations had been thought of prior to 1974. In fact, a modest attempt to achieve a small working group along these lines had been tried in 1973-1974, but eventually lost momentum and disbanded. However, by the end of 1974, the time was ripe for another try at forming such a working coalition. The increasing politicization of Title IX issues, in particular, highlighted the need to form a united front to lobby Congress and pressure DHEW. The structure of the initial coalition established in 1974 was extremely informal and the purpose was almost exclusively information sharing between the dozen participants. By 1976 this group (now identified as the National Coalition for Women and Girls in Education) had become much more formally organized, although not legally incorporated, and had expanded to include representatives of over forty organizations.

Although the original purpose of information sharing remains the primary purpose of the Coalition, it has now expanded its activities to include direct political and legal action. The Coalition's activities in opposing legislative proposals—such as those introduced by Casey, Tower, Holt, and O'Hara—and in supporting adequate funding for the Women's Educational Equity Act have been highly successful. The Coalition's efforts were also instrumental in bringing about some of the changes made by the White House in the Title IX regulation developed by DHEW. The Coalition has been less successful in getting DHEW to enforce Title IX more strictly, but the pressure from this group has resulted in some improvements in DHEW's regulation implementation effort.

The Coalition's movement into the political arena has created problems for some of the participants who work for organizations that oppose the Coalition's positions. As a result, the amount and type of involvement of the participants varies widely and changes from issue to issue. For the most part, a small core of the Coalition's membership provides the impetus for its direction and activities. Not surprisingly, the more active members are those who are in positions that allow them to work exclusively on women's education issues. The establishment of projects on women's education—such as the Association of American Colleges' Project on the Status and Education of Women and NOW's Legal Defense and Education Fund's Project on Equal Education Rights—has resulted in the availability of substantial staff and secretarial support to direct the operation of the Coalition.

Private foundation support for these two projects, as well as other similar projects, has helped to create a work base in Washington of dedicated and knowledgeable people who serve as full-time monitors of all activities relating to sex discrimination in education. Previously, women who were interested in this area had to volunteer their own time and generally had no staff or monetary support. As a result of this financial and staffing change, the scope and efficacy of the actions taken has increased significantly. The prevailing work pattern has always been and continues to be one of extreme dedication combined with a willingness to labor long and hard. Progress towards the achievement of women's education equity has been advanced greatly as a result of the conviction of purpose displayed by these people. Because so many intelligent, educated, and skilled women are knowledgeable and interested in the field of education, the topic of sex discrimination in education has become a clearly defined component of the larger women's rights movement. As a result, education has been an area that has received more attention and seen more progress than many other social and economic problem areas of concern to feminists.

The diversity of the organizations that comprise the Coalition is one of its major strengths: Due to their different perspectives, there is an extensive cross-fertilization of ideas. Membership in the Coalition also has an effect on the individual organizations by helping to influence and shape the separate priorities and agendas of these bodies. However, the diversity of the membership organizations also creates problems for the Coalition when it attempts to establish a unified strategy and decide on a joint action. Some of the participants represent broad-based, multi-purpose groups such as the National Organization for Women, League of Women Voters, and National Women's Political Caucus. Other participants work for narrow, single-interest groups, such as the National

Association for Girls and Women in Sports and Association for Intercollegiate Athletics for Women. As a result, there is sometimes conflict over which topics the participants believe that the Coalition should address and the importance it should attach to different issues. There is also a difference in perspective between those participants who work for organizations mainly concerned with education policy—such as the National Student Lobby, National Education Association, and American Council on Education—and those who represent groups that are concerned generally with the treatment of women in society— such as Women's Lobby, Women's Equity Action League, and Women's Legal Defense Fund. The cohesion and unity of purpose of the Coalition is sometimes strained as a result of the varied nature of its membership, although overall the diversity has proven to be an asset.

The Coalition is somewhat unusual for an organization concerned with women's rights in that it has minority-oriented groups among its members. Represented in the Coalition are such groups as the League of United Latin American Citizens, National Council of La Raza, Lawyers' Committee for Civil Rights Under Law, National Council of Negro Women and National Urban League. Not only does the Coalition receive input from groups concerned primarily with the rights of minorities, but the Coalition has worked hard to establish a working relationship between other civil rights and women's rights groups. It was the lobbying activities on the Holt amendment, which threatened the rights of both women and minorities, that initially encouraged these groups to work together. Previously, these civil rights and women's groups had considered their interests to be at best separate, and at worst, conflicting. The relationship and organizational communications that were established while working against the Holt amendment became stronger as a result of the combined effort to block the DHEW-proposed regulation concerning civil rights enforcement procedures. While the cooperation between women's and other civil rights groups remains loosely organized, for the first time there exists a broad coalition of women and minority groups acting in harmony to influence legislative and executive actions. If the organizational and ideological differences separating these groups can continue to be bridged over issues of mutual interest, then the strength of both the women's coalition and the minority coalition will be greatly enhanced, and their impact on national politics will increase as a result.

Future Efforts to End Sex Bias in Education

With the enactment of the Women's Education Equity Act and Title IX, the legislative foundation for a major federal program to end sex bias in education has been established. As a result of the passage of these laws, sex discrimination in almost every aspect of education has been made illegal, and a program has been established to fund projects aimed at hastening the process of change in the treatment by schools of girls and women. Due to the passage of these laws, the involvement of Congress in the future can be expected to be more limited than in the past. The role of Congress will probably be restricted to considering narrowly focused amendments to limit the impact of Title IX in a particular area. In addition, Congress will have to decide whether to extend the Women's Educational Equity, and if so, at what funding level. Congress will also be called upon to make changes in specific education programs in terms of their impact on sex-role stereotyping and the perpetuation of sex discrimination. With these exceptions, the main responsibility at the national level for dealing with issues relating to sex bias in education will be the responsibility of the executive branch.

Because of the low level of funding it has received, the impact of the Women's Educational Equity Act will remain limited and of only marginal consequence. In contrast, the methods and extent to which DHEW enforces Title IX will remain a major factor in determining the pace at which schools and colleges eliminate biased policies and practices. In addition, DHEW has the potential to serve as a major change agent if it decides to make the elimination of sex discrimination a major departmental objective. Equitable treatment for women could be a criteria to be considered when making grants and taken into account when reviewing the operation of federally assisted education programs, thus bringing the full force of DHEW's funding to bear on the problem of sex discrimination. If this is not done, then the Office for Civil Rights will remain the exclusive forum for challenging sexist policies—a responsibility too large for it at present to handle adequately. As a result, disputes over the meaning of the Title IX regulation and the best procedures to be followed in obtaining compliance with its requirements will dominate the national scene.

The role the federal courts will play can be expected to increase as more and more individuals turn to them to achieve a redress of grievances. How helpful the courts will be in resolving sex discrimination disputes is unclear, since the legal status to be given complaints of sex discrimination has not yet been resolved. Still, the potential for winning court cases that have nationwide implications will make litigation an attractive strategy for women seeking to have a broad impact on school policies. The possible passage of the Equal Rights Amendment would obviously accelerate positive court action.

While the first part of the 1970s was mainly a time period characterized by national political action challenging sex discrimination in education, during the remainder of the decade there can be expected to be a shift in emphasis back to the state and local levels. It will be at these governmental levels where the specific policy issues concerning school policies will be raised and where the discord between women's, students', and parents' groups and school officials will take place. The decentralization of conflict over school policy from Washington to the state and local levels will create a second and substantially different phase in the movement to end sex bias in education. This phase will place a new and greater burden on organizations such as the League of Women Voters, National Organization for Women, and the American Association of University Women, which have local affiliates throughout the country, to provide leadership and direction for their state and local groups. The performance of these types of groups at the state and local levels will determine the progress made toward combatting sexism in the schools. While a relatively few women in Washington have been able to achieve significant results to protect and advance the rights of women in education during the past years, in the future it will take thousands of concerned parents, students, and educators throughout the country to bring about meaningful change. Whether or not there is sufficient grass-roots interests in altering the treatment of girls and women by the education system will determine the extent to which the successes achieved at the national level are actually translated into program and policy changes at the local school and college levels. These local policy changes are vitally necessary in order to establish complete and total educational equity for girls and women.

Index

Abzug, Bella, 101
Academic women, discrimination against, 11-12, 14
Advisory Committee on the Rights and Responsibilities of Women: creation of, 3; position on Women's Educational Equity Act, 77; recommendations leading to Title IX, 95, 96, 97, 98
Advisory Council on Women's Educational Programs, DHEW: activities of, 65, 84-85, 86, 87, 88; legislation to create, 69, 71, 73
Affirmative action. See Executive Order 11246
Age Discrimination Act of 1975, 145n
American Association of University Women, 68, 125, 154
American Civil Liberties Union (ACLU), 28, 40, 146
American Council on Education, 73, 152
American Federation of Teachers (AFT), 40, 148
American Jewish Congress, 40
American Medical Women's Association, 6
American Personnel and Guidance Association, 73
Amicus briefs, 37, 40-41, 146-149
Assistant Secretary for Education, DHEW, 54, 55, 62, 85, 108, 110
Assistant Secretary for Planning and Evaluation, DHEW, 108, 110
Association of American Colleges, 73, 75; Project on the Status and Education of Women, 151
Association for Intercollegiate Athletics for Women, 152
Association of Junior Leagues, 7
Association for Supervision and Curriculum Development, 73
Athletics: coverage under Title IX, 82, 109, 112, 113, 114, 116, 119, 123, 124, 127, 134; sex discrimination in, 11, 15. See also Physical education

Bayh, Birch, 98, 99, 100, 102, 117, 118, 138
Beauty contests, coverage under Title IX, 126
Blackman, Harry, 43
Boards of Education. See School boards
Boy Scouts, coverage under Title IX, 109, 110
Boys' State programs, coverage under Title IX, 126, 131

Brademas, John, 97, 100
Brennan, William, 43
Brigham Young University, 128
Burger, Warren, 42, 43

California, amicus brief filed by, 40-41
Cannon, Walter, 99
Carmichael, Stokely, 4
Casey, Robert, 120, 125-126, 150
Chamber of Commerce, U.S., 41
Chesterfield County, community involvement in Cohen case, 26, 34-35, 45-46
Chesterfield Education Association (CEA), 26, 33
Citizens' Advisory Council on Status of Women, 32
Civil Rights Act of 1957, 98
Civil Rights Act of 1964: basis for maternity leave case, 28, 32, 40; model for Title IX, 96, 97, 98, 100, 106, 107, 109; passage of, 3; OCR enforcement of, 144, 145n
Civil rights movement, 4
Classification Act of 1923, 2
Coalition of Labor Union Women, 6
Cohen, Leo, 23
Cohen, Susan, 23-48, 146, 147
Cohen v. Chesterfield County, 23-48
College admission policies, coverage under Title IX, 97, 98, 99, 100, 101, 103, 134. See also Single sex colleges
Commission on Civil Rights, U.S., 84, 96, 101, 150
Commissioner of Education, DHEW: responsibilities under Special Projects Act, 80, 81, 84, 85; role in approving Title IX transition plans, 108; role in having OE study sex discrimination, 49, 50, 55, 56, 57, 58, 59
Commissioner's Task Force on the Impact of Office of Education Programs on Women, OE; 49-66; impact on passage of Women's Educational Equity Act, 73-74, 76, 77
Comprehensive Alcohol Abuse and Alcoholism Prevention, Treatment and Rehabilitation Act of 1970, 145n
Congress: overview of involvement on sex discrimination issues, 132-133, 137-141, 152-153; procedures to veto regulations, 114, 121-125. See also House of Representatives; Senate; and names of individual Committees, Subcommittees and members of Congress

155

About the Authors

Andrew Fishel received his doctorate in American politics and education from Columbia University. He is a policy analyst in the Office of the Secretary, U.S. Department of Health, Education and Welfare.

Janice Pottker is completing the Ph.D. in sociology and education at Columbia University. She is Director of the Center for the Study of Sex Differences in Education, Bethesda, Maryland and is currently conducting a project grant funded under the Women's Educational Equity Act for the U.S. Office of Education.

The authors have previously collaborated on an anthology entitled *Sex Bias In The Schools: The Research Evidence*, (Fairleigh Dickinson University Press). They have also authored and coauthored numerous articles on sex discrimination in education that have appeared in *Journal of Higher Education, Integrated Education, Educational Researcher, Educational Forum*, and *Contemporary Education*. In addition, they have presented papers on sexism in education at the annual meetings of the American Sociological Association and American Educational Research Association.

Holly Knox is Director of the Project on Equal Education Rights (PEER) of the NOW Legal Defense and Education Fund. Created in 1974, PEER is monitoring enforcement progress under federal law barring sex discrimination in education. A former legislative specialist in DHEW, Knox chaired the Office of Education's Task Force on the Impact of Office of Education Programs on Women.

Mary Ann Millsap is a senior evaluation specialist in the Dissemination and Resources Group in the National Institute of Education. She was previously a program analyst in the Office of Planning, Budgeting, and Evaluation, U.S. Office of Education.